AF580859

Foreign Aid Allocation, Governance, and Economic Growth

This book is published by the University of Pennsylvania Press (UPP) on behalf of the International Food Policy Research Institute (IFPRI) as part of a joint-publication series. Books in the series present research on food security and economic development with the aim of reducing poverty and eliminating hunger and malnutrition in developing nations. They are the product of peer-reviewed IFPRI research and are selected by mutual agreement between the parties for publication under the joint IFPRI-UPP imprint.

Foreign Aid Allocation, Governance, and Economic Growth

KAMILJON T. AKRAMOV

Published for the International Food Policy Research Institute

University of Pennsylvania Press
Philadelphia

Published by
University of Pennsylvania Press
Philadelphia, Pennsylvania 19104-4112
www.upenn.edu/pennpress

Library of Congress Cataloging-in-Publication Data

Akramov, Kamil.
Foreign aid allocation, governance, and economic growth / Kamiljon T. Akramov. — 1st ed.
p. cm. — (International Food Policy Research Institute)
Includes bibliographical references and index.
ISBN 978-0-8122-4465-6 (hardcover : alk. paper)
1. Economic assistance—Developing countries—Evaluation. 2. Economic development—Social aspects—Developing countries. 3. Economic indicators—Developing countries. 4. Developing countries—Economic conditions. I. Title. II. Series: International Food Policy Research Institute (Series)
HC59.7.A752 2012
338.9109172'4—dc23 2012004087

Printed in the United States of America on acid-free paper
10 9 8 7 6 5 4 3 2 1

Contents

Figures

Tables

Foreword

Both bilateral and multilateral donors have increased their official development assistance (ODA) from its levels at the start of the twenty-first century. The combined effect of these aid increases has been to raise ODA by nearly 80 percent in real terms since 2000, and total net ODA flows reached about US$130 billion in 2010—the highest real ODA level in history. Although development outcomes are largely determined by the less developed countries themselves, foreign development assistance can provide such countries with additional resources to enhance their development prospects and promote economic growth and poverty reduction. The existing empirical literature is ambiguous as to whether foreign aid promotes economic growth in recipient countries, however, and it provides widely divergent estimates of the cross-country relationship between foreign aid flows and economic growth rates. This book by Kamiljon Akramov contributes to the literature by examining whether sectoral aid allocation patterns impact ODA's effectiveness in promoting economic growth in aid-recipient countries.

The author concludes that historical factors such as colonial links and language traits, donors' geopolitical and commercial interests, and the relative size of the recipient play important roles in determining the amount of aid allocated.

Using various econometric models, the study further concludes that aid for economic uses—including aid to production sectors and economic infrastructure—promotes long-term economic growth in aid-recipient countries due to a positive impact on domestic investment. The findings also suggest that this impact is not conditional on how democratic the recipient government is. These findings are particularly significant given that donors have been allocating less aid (measured both in real dollar value and as a share of total ODA) for economic uses since the 1990s. In particular, aid to the production sectors (including agriculture, industry, and trade) decreased by about threefold, dropping from a high of about 28–29 percent in the early 1980s to less than 10 percent in the 2000s.

Shenggen Fan
Director General, International Food Policy Research Institute

Acknowledgments

I am grateful to Regina Birner, Tom Epley, Shenggen Fan, Johan Fedderke, Gershon Feder, Yi Feng, Jacob Klerman, Robert Klitgaard, Sergey Mahnovski, Margaret McMillan, Rachel Swanger, Clay Wescott, Charles Wolf, two anonymous reviewers, the Publications Review Committee of the International Food Policy Research Institute (IFPRI), and participants in seminars held at the Asian Development Bank, IFPRI, and the RAND Corporation. I also thank John Whitehead for his excellent editorial help and suggestions, and Corinne Garber and Gwendolyn Stansbury for their support throughout the process.

The research for this book was supported by the United States Agency for International Development through the Initiative to End Hunger in Africa. Part of the research was supported by the Pardee RAND Graduate School in Santa Monica, California, through the Palevsky Fellowship Award. I am grateful to both organizations for their financial support. The opinions and claims expressed herein do not necessarily reflect the views of the organizations and individuals listed.

Acronyms and Abbreviations

2SLS	two-stage least squares
3SLS	three-stage least squares
AP	Angrist and Pischke (2009)
CPIA	Country Policy and Institutional Assessment
CRS	Credit Reporting System
DAC	Development Assistance Committee
DDD	difference-in-difference-in-differences
DFID	UK Department for International Development
DV	dependent variable
EC	European Commission
FDI	foreign direct investment
FGLS	feasible generalized least squares
GDP	gross domestic product
GMM	generalized method of moments
GNI	gross national income
ICRG	International Country Risk Guide
IDA	International Development Association
IV	instrumental variable
LIML	limited information, maximum likelihood
ODA	official development assistance
OECD	Organisation for Economic Co-operation and Development
OLS	ordinary least squares
RET	random-effects tobit
SE-IV	single-equation instrumental variable
SSA	Sub-Saharan Africa
SSE-IV	simultaneous system of equations instrumental variable
UNDP	United Nations Development Programme
UNESCAP	United Nations Economic and Social Commission for Asia and the Pacific

Foreign Aid Allocation, Governance, and Economic Growth

1 Introduction

In 2010, the total net official development assistance flows from members of the Development Assistance Committee of the Organisation for Economic Co-operation and Development (OECD) rose to US$128.7 billion, the highest real dollar figure ever recorded, reflecting a general scaling up of foreign aid (OECD 2011).[1] Although the scaling up of foreign aid seems to bring hope and the prospect of a better future for the poor in developing countries, it will also raise many challenges. Can foreign development assistance help promote pro-poor growth and poverty reduction in developing countries? Is there any evidence that foreign aid causes greater economic growth in recipient countries? These are important questions for the development community, because each year donors transfer tens of billions of dollars in development assistance to developing countries. The heated debate over whether foreign aid is effective in promoting development outcomes has been ongoing for decades among development economists, aid practitioners, and policymakers. There are two competing perspectives. One argues that although foreign aid has occasionally failed, it has promoted economic development and poverty reduction in many low-income countries and prevented worse outcomes in others, and therefore, ending poverty requires a significant increase in development assistance (Sachs 2005). Another perspective argues that aid is part of the problem rather than the solution to the problems of less developed countries (Easterly 2006).

Despite voluminous empirical literature devoted to the aid–growth relationship, the answer to the question of whether foreign aid has any causal benefits remains unclear. One group of studies suggests that aid has *a conditional positive impact on growth,* promoting economic growth only in certain conditions. An influential study by Burnside and Dollar (2000) argues that aid can be effective in a good policy environment. However, Easterly, Levine, and Roodman (2004) argue that the results of Burnside and Dollar (2000) are not robust and that there is no strong evidence of the effectiveness of foreign aid even in a good policy environment. More recently, Rajan and Subramanian

1. All dollar amounts in the book are US dollars unless otherwise indicated. All monetary amounts used in the book's calculations are in constant (real) US dollars.

(2008) used cross-sectional instrumental variables and dynamic panel regressions to examine the effects of aid on economic growth. Their results suggest that there is no statistically significant "positive (or negative) relationship between aid flows into a country and its economic growth" (643). Further, Kourtellos, Tan, and Zhang (2007) used a sample-splitting econometric technique that allows one to simultaneously control for the existence of heterogeneity and nonlinearity. Their results suggest that foreign aid is potentially counterproductive to economic growth. In this regard, the literature suggests that foreign aid probably comes with severe side effects, such as causing real exchange rate appreciation (an effect known as "Dutch disease"), disappearing into unproductive government consumption, inducing rent seeking, and adversely influencing legal and economic institutions (Remmer 2004; Rajan and Subramanian 2005, 2007; Heckelman and Knack 2008).

On the contrary, another group of studies suggests that foreign aid, in all likelihood, positively influences economic growth but has diminishing returns, and its effect is unconditional to policy environment (Dalgaard and Hansen 2000; Hansen and Tarp 2001; Dalgaard, Hansen, and Tarp 2004). More recently, Arndt, Jones, and Tarp (2010), using a modified version of the instrumentation strategy of Rajan and Subramanian (2008), re-examined the aid–growth relationship. Their results suggest that aid has a positive and statistically significant causal effect on growth over the long run. They conclude that "aid has been and remains a key tool for enhancing the development prospects of poor nations" (2010, 24).

One of the increasingly popular directions in the literature is to examine the impact of disaggregated aid on development outcomes. A study by Clemens, Radelet, and Bhavnani (2004) disaggregating aid by the timing of impact finds that "short-impact" aid (about 53 percent of all aid flows) has a significant positive and causal effect on economic growth. Mishra and Newhouse (2009) reveal a small but statistically significant effect of health aid on infant mortality. Similarly, Dreber, Nunnenkamp, and Thiele (2008), using panel data, find that a higher level of per capita aid for education has a statistically significant positive impact on primary school enrollment. Nevertheless, we know very little about the differential impacts of different aid categories on economic growth. Given that donors focus on multidimensional objectives in their aid allocation decisions, a more disaggregated approach to the analysis of the aid–growth relationship is desirable.

This study attempts to contribute to this debate by investigating whether sectoral aid allocation patterns influence the effectiveness of foreign aid in promoting economic growth. The starting proposition is that different components of aid may have different transmission channels in their impact on growth. Foreign aid is disaggregated into three mutually exclusive and collectively exhaustive categories: (1) aid for economic uses (or economic aid), including aid to production sectors and economic infrastructure; (2) aid for social uses (or social aid), including aid for education, health, water, and sanitation; and (3) other aid, including emergency aid, food aid, and so forth. Then, focusing on the first two categories of aid, which account for nearly two-thirds of all aid flows, the empirical aid effectiveness and allocation models are estimated. One empirical assumption is that economic aid affects growth mainly through its impact on physical capital accumulation (domestic investment). Overall, one may expect that if economic aid supplements domestic resources, its impact on domestic investment should be positive. However, if economic aid substitutes for domestic resources rather than supplementing them, its impact could be insignificant or even negative. In addition, it is assumed that the part of economic aid that goes to economic infrastructure may also affect economic growth by improving efficiency and enhancing total factor productivity. This might be the case if improvements in public infrastructure reduce the transaction costs of production in the private sector.

Further, the intent of social aid is to create and improve human capital in recipient countries, for example, by supporting public education or primary healthcare. Therefore, it is plausible to propose that this part of aid may impact economic growth by creating additional human capital. The study also assumes that the magnitude and direction of the previously mentioned impact channels of foreign aid on economic growth could be affected by the quality of governance in a given recipient country. Therefore, the study examines whether the quality of democratic governance is a significant factor in aid effectiveness by looking at how the measures of democratic governance interact with sectoral aid components. The measure of democratic governance used in this study is a combination of the political rights and civil liberties indicators of Freedom House.

In these ways, the study improves on and extends the instrumentation strategy most recently used in the literature on aid effectiveness. This allows it to provide causal evidence that aid for economic uses promotes long-term growth in aid-recipient countries through its significant positive impact on domestic investment. This impact is unconditional to the level of democratic governance. The regression results obtained using the instrumental variables approach in the framework of a system of simultaneous equations suggest that the ratio of investment to gross domestic product (GDP) has a positive causal impact on the long-term average growth rates of per capita GDP, with an estimated coefficient of 0.12. In turn, the result for the investment equation shows a statistically significant positive relationship between economic aid and domestic investment with an estimated coefficient of 2.17. Combining these two results shows that a 1 percentage point increase in the ratio of economic aid to GDP increases the long-run per capita growth rate by 0.27 percent. These results are essentially supported by the qualitatively similar results of dynamic panel, both the difference generalized method of moments (GMM) and the system GMM regressions. These findings are consistent with theoretical and empirical literature.

The study is closely related to several existing studies. First, in using mainly donor-related determinants of foreign aid for the instrumentation of the ratio of aid to GDP, this study is similar to recent work by Rajan and Subramanian (2008) and Arndt, Jones, and Tarp (2010). Rajan and Subramanian (2008) exploit the fact that aid is often extended for historical reasons (colonial links). They also use donor size relative to that of the recipient as a scale factor. Arndt, Jones, and Tarp (2010) introduced several changes to this instrumentation strategy by excluding suspect variables, introducing donor-specific fixed effects, and using aid per capita as a dependent variable in place of the ratio of aid to GDP. The instrumentation strategy used in this study further extends this approach by considering political similarities between donors and recipients as well as donors' strategic and commercial interests as exogenous determinants of foreign aid. It also makes some additional modifications to account for differences in sectoral aid allocations. Second, the study is related to broad empirical literature that explores the question of how foreign aid is allocated among recipient countries (for example, Trumbull and Wall 1994; Alesina and Dollar 2000; Berthélemy and Tichit 2004; Fleck and Kilby 2010). Third, it is related to studies such as Svensson (2000a) and Kosack (2003) that have found that democratic governance can encourage a more productive use of foreign aid. However, different from those studies, it finds that the interactions of democratic governance either with aggregate aid or with its different components are not significant. These results are similar to the findings of the study by Dreber, Nunnenkamp, and Thiele (2008). Fourth, this study is related to recent studies that examine the impacts of different categories of aid on development outcomes (Clemens, Radelet, and Bhavnani 2004; Dreber, Nunnenkamp, and Thiele 2008; Mishra and Newhouse 2009). This study differs from those studies in that it examines the differential impact of foreign aid in a more comprehensive manner. Finally, the study benefited a great deal from methodological approaches used by Frankel and Romer (1999); Acemoglu, Johnson, and Robinson (2001); and Rajan and Subramanian (2008).

The rest of the book is organized as follows. Chapter 2 provides an overview of previous literature relating to foreign aid, governance, and the relation of aid to economic development. Chapter 3 describes the sources of data and discusses the patterns of foreign aid flows over the past five decades. Chapter 4 discusses theoretical and empirical issues related to aid allocation, then provides the empirical results. The analytical framework related to the analysis of the aid–growth relationship, econometric estimation, issues and instrumentation strategy is discussed in Chapter 5. This chapter also reports the empirical results obtained using cross-sectional and dynamic panel regression methods. The final chapter of the book summarizes the main findings and draws conclusions.

2 Overview of Previous Studies

The community of donors has now accumulated more than five decades of experience in providing aid to developing countries. The objectives, strategies and policies, amount, and composition of foreign aid to developing countries have changed substantially over time. Although in the early years it was expected that the need for foreign assistance would decline as private capital became available to developing countries, official foreign assistance has remained the most important source of external financing for most developing countries. Although international flows of private capital to developing countries have increased significantly in recent years, the bulk of these flows are concentrated in a few countries that have particular attractions from investors' point of view.[1] Therefore, the majority of developing countries, especially those with low incomes and limited export earnings and without access to international private capital markets, continue to depend on concessional flows to supplement their domestic capital accumulation and to sustain their development efforts.

Literature on foreign aid documents that two important developments—political factors and the progress of development thinking—have made crucial impacts on the evolution of contemporary development assistance (Hjertholm and White 2000; Kanbur 2000, 2006). Although the need for foreign aid was initially justified as a moral responsibility of the rich countries to the poor, donor ideology over decades has been influenced by political factors and changed frequently from one objective to another. In the 1960s and 1970s, donors mainly focused on nation-building, promoting production capacity, and meeting basic human needs. Then, during the 1980s, donors' focus shifted to

1. According to the World Bank (2012), net international flows of private capital to developing countries reached $1.06 trillion in 2010, including equity ($635 billion) and debt ($424 billion) inflows. The largest component of equity inflows is foreign direct investment (FDI), which stood at $506 billion in 2010. However, the bulk of these flows go to a few highly attractive emerging economies. For example, more than 70 percent of the total net equity inflows to developing countries in 2010 went to seven emerging economies: Brazil, China, India, Mexico, the Russian Federation, and Turkey.

macroeconomic stabilization, structural adjustment, and debt reduction. In the 1990s, donors provided considerable support to political and economic transition in Eastern Europe and the former Soviet Union. During that period, donors also started to focus on poverty reduction and social infrastructure, including health and education (Hjertholm and White 2000). During the past decade (that is, after 2000), donors started to put more emphasis on performance-based aid allocation, focusing on the Millennium Development Goals, global health (HIV/AIDs), governance, and security. The progress in development thinking also made a significant impact on the evolution of foreign aid policies over the past five or six decades.[2]

This study crosses the boundaries of three branches of the literature. Since donors started providing foreign assistance to developing countries, a broad empirical literature has emerged to examine the impact of foreign aid on development outcomes as well as determinants of foreign aid. This substantial and growing body of research has dramatically increased our knowledge of how aid affects developing economies and what factors determine donors' aid allocation decisions. In addition, this literature has introduced a variety of innovative techniques for dealing with the estimation inherent in evaluating development effectiveness. It would be vastly beyond the scope of this book to provide a detailed review and critique of hundreds of studies that have analyzed donors' aid allocation policies and aid effectiveness. Instead, to develop a better understanding of the previous findings and methodological issues related to the topic, this study summarizes the major results and weaknesses of previous studies. It starts with a review of the literature on aid effectiveness focusing on whether foreign aid promotes economic growth in recipient countries. Then it provides a brief overview of studies on determinants of foreign aid flows. A rapidly growing literature on governance and growth describes how the quality of governance and institutions can affect economic growth. The final section of this chapter provides an overview of this literature.

Aid Effectiveness: What Do We Know?

The role and function of foreign aid have been influenced by and thus have to be evaluated in the light of development thinking. In fact, economic theory has been influential in identifying criteria for examination of aid effectiveness. Since the early years, the criterion for aid effectiveness has been whether aid is effective in promoting economic development and welfare in recipient countries. This criterion has been explored from different methodological and ideological perspectives. Studies have evaluated aid effectiveness at both the micro- and macroeconomic levels, relying on both cross-country comparisons and

2. An overview of trends in the relationship between development thinking and foreign aid is provided in Appendix A.

single-country case studies and using broad surveys of qualitative and multi-disciplinary analysis as well as empirical analytical studies. A complete survey of aid effectiveness studies is neither a feasible nor an essential task for this study. Instead I focus on summarizing the main results and weaknesses of the empirical studies on aid effectiveness.

Before moving to the review of empirical studies on aid effectiveness, I briefly summarize two alternative views regarding the potential impact of foreign aid on economic development. On the one hand, proponents of foreign assistance to developing countries argue that most poor developing countries lack domestic savings to finance existing profitable investment opportunities and have limited or no access to international private capital markets; therefore, official foreign assistance could play an important role (as the only source in many developing countries) in filling the financing gap in order to attain a needed investment level and targeted growth rate (Chenery and Strout 1966). Contemporary proponents of foreign aid (Stern 2002; Stiglitz 2002; Sachs 2005) argue that although aid has sometimes failed, it has prevented worse performance in many countries and even supported poverty reduction and successful development efforts in several others, citing examples including the Green Revolution in Asia, eradication of various infectious diseases as a result of the Global Alliance for Vaccines and Immunization, the success of export processing zones in East Asia, and so forth.

On the other hand, some influential economists argue that the objectives of foreign aid are worthwhile but its premises are wrong and it would be a waste of money (Friedman 1958; Little and Clifford 1965; Bauer 1986). They also argue that aid flows have largely contributed or will contribute to the failure of development efforts in many developing countries by enlarging government bureaucracies, perpetuating rent-seeking and corruption, and enriching the elites in poor countries. According to Easterly (2003, 2007), one of the strong contemporary critics of foreign aid, there is too much corruption in recipient countries and unaccountability in aid delivery mechanisms. He claims, therefore, that foreign aid has done much bad and little good in recipient countries and argues against upscaling foreign aid flows.

Early empirical studies on aid effectiveness mainly used the framework of the Harrod-Domar growth model and two-gap models, in which the incremental ratio of capital to output is a key determinant of economic growth. Assuming that there is a savings gap that constrains investment and growth, these studies emphasized the role of aid in financing investment and proposed a causal link running from aid to savings to investment to growth. The evidence in this regard overwhelmingly suggests that there is a negative relationship between foreign aid and domestic savings. The reason is that the marginal propensity of savings is always less than one and the marginal propensity of consumption is always above zero. Therefore, when income rises as a result of foreign assistance, part of the additional income goes to current consumption, so savings increases by less than the value of aid flows. Further foreign aid displaces domestic savings, and in this sense aid has a negative influence on savings (Hansen and Tarp 2000).

There are two problems with this argument. First, the reasoning used earlier is static in nature and ignores potential feedback from higher income to future higher savings and higher growth. Second, the bulk of foreign assistance goes to health and education, which are considered consumer goods but help to build human capital, which in turn plays an important role in future savings, investment, and economic growth. Therefore, the results of static analyses that show that foreign aid has a negative or insignificant effect on savings are flawed on methodological grounds (White 1992, 1998).

The aid–investment relationship has also received noteworthy attention from researchers from academia and international financial institutions. Overall, the available studies seem to indicate that there is a positive relationship between foreign aid and domestic investment in recipient countries. Hansen and Tarp (2000) summarize the results of 29 earlier studies that attempted to test the proposition that asserts that foreign aid stimulates domestic investment. Their meta-analysis provides overwhelming support for the proposition that aid helps to increase the investment ratio in recipient countries, with 15 out of 16 estimates providing a positive and statistically significant result. For example, Levy (1987) showed that the estimated coefficient of aid with respect to domestic investment was approximately 0.86, thus suggesting that an increase of 1 percentage point in the ratio of aid to income leads to an increase of 0.86 percentage point in the investment ratio.[3] Lensink and Morrissey (2000), in a cross-sectional study of 75 aid recipient countries, also found that aid has a positive and statistically significant impact on investment. Furthermore, Hansen and Tarp (2001), in a panel data analysis of 56 developing countries, obtained similar results.

Dollar and Easterly (1999) investigated the relationship between foreign aid and domestic investment country by country for the period 1965–95. They found that out of 88 aid recipient countries for which they performed the analysis, the relationship between aid and investment was negative and significant in 36 countries, negative but insignificant in 17 countries, positive and significant in 23 countries, and positive but insignificant in 12 countries. However, they investigated the relationship between the ratio of official development assistance (ODA) to GDP and the ratio of investment to GDP using a simple ordinary least squares (OLS) model and did not control for potential sources of bias, and therefore their results should be taken with precaution, but they still suggest that there is heterogeneity in the relationship between aid and investment across aid recipient countries.

3. When aid net of technical assistance is used, the coefficient rises to 0.96. This highlights the notion about the heterogeneity of different aid flows and the importance of aid disaggregation in evaluating the impact of aid on development outcomes.

Later the focus shifted away from the simplistic Harrod-Domar and two-gap models toward more sophisticated models based on the neoclassical growth model, as well as on other growth models, and most of the academic and policy debate on aid effectiveness focused on the *relationship between aid and growth* despite the fact that a substantial part of foreign assistance is not primarily intended to support growth. Some of the studies based on these models estimated the impact of aid on the presumption that only temporary aid can increase investment and permanent aid merely increases consumption and does not increase investment, hence growth. Others assumed that aid can help a recipient country to reduce poverty or even to escape from a "poverty trap" onto a higher steady-state growth path. A more sophisticated theoretical framework also led some researchers to emphasize human capital, policies, and institutional factors that may support or constrain growth.

This new approach produced a broad but contradictory literature on the aid–growth relationship.[4] There is no agreement on the effects of aid. Some authors argue that aid helps to promote growth and structural adjustment in many less developed countries, while others oppose it. As stressed by many authors, a review of the results of these studies suggests three competing observations on the aid–growth relationship (Radelet 2006).

The results of the first group of studies imply that *foreign aid has no effect on growth and may sometimes even undermine growth* in recipient countries. The most widely cited earlier studies on aid effectiveness that found a negative relationship between aid and growth are those by Mosley, Hudson, and Horrel (1987, 1992). Using both cross-sectional and time-series analyses, they found that foreign aid does not stimulate economic growth. They explained these results in terms of the possible leakage of aid into nonproductive expenditure in the public sector and the transmission of a negative price effect into the private sector.

An important study by Boone (1994) also concluded that there is no significant relationship between aid and growth.[5] It also suggested that aid neither creates nor correlates with those fundamental factors that cause growth. This and other studies with similar findings have suggested the crowding out of private investment and savings, the "Dutch disease" effect, corruption, embezzlement, and rent-seeking behavior among a variety of reasons that aid might not promote economic growth. However, Ovaska (2003) argues that there is no considerable evidence that development aid is effective in promoting economic growth in developing countries even with better governance.

The results of studies by Mosley, Hudson, and Horrel (1987, 1992) and Boone (1994) and other similar studies have been fairly criticized on the grounds of their underlying structural model and econometric methodology. Their results

---

4. Hansen and Tarp (2001) estimate that from the 1970s to 2000 no fewer than 72 cross-country studies tested the link between aid and growth in reduced-form equations.

5. This study was cited in the *Economist* on December 10, 1994, with the intriguing headline "Aid Down the Rathole."

were mainly based on simple OLS regressions and assumed only a simple linear relationship between aid and growth.[6] Besides these critiques, another important criticism of Boone (1994) is the use of a static model over a 20-year period, which does not allow dynamics of adjustment.

Furthermore, in a recent study Rajan and Subramanian (2008), using cross-sectional instrumental variable (IV) and panel GMM regressions analysis, found no robust evidence of a positive (or negative) relationship between aid flows into a country and its economic growth, with their conclusion holding across time periods and types of aid. They also found no evidence that aid is more effective in better policy environments. Their main idea for instrumentation was to model the supply of aid by using noneconomic factors that drive donors to provide development assistance to recipient countries. In this way, their instrument accounted for historic relationships between donors and recipients based on colonial links and commonality of languages, as well as the potential influence of the donor's and recipient's relative population sizes. The interactions between colonial links and relative population sizes were also included in the construction of Rajan and Subramanian's complicated instrument. However, Bazzi and Clemens (2009) questioned the validity of this instrument and showed that the instrument used by Rajan and Subramanian contains very little information beyond the recipient population size. Because recipient population size might affect growth through other channels, such as trade, Bazzi and Clemens argue that the Rajan and Subramanian (2008) results face serious questions concerning the validity of the instrument.

Kourtellos, Tan, and Zhang (2007) examined the relationship between foreign aid and growth using more advanced econometric techniques—sample-splitting methods—that allowed them to simultaneously account for the existence of heterogeneity and nonlinearity and address model uncertainty. Their results also suggested that foreign aid is potentially counterproductive to economic growth. In this regard, Rajan and Subramanian (2007) suggested that one of the possible channels by which aid might adversely affect growth is the association of aid with poor governance, reducing the need for government to generate domestic revenues or enlist cooperation from the governed. The study suggests that "even if the paucity of capital is the missing ingredient in the process of setting countries on the path to prosperity, the form in which the capital is received could have adverse spillover effects that limit its value" (Rajan and Subramanian 2007, 326).

The literature has suggested various reasons for the failure of foreign aid to promote growth in aid recipient countries: foreign aid probably comes with severe side effects, such as causing real exchange appreciation ("Dutch disease"), disappearing into unproductive government consumption, inducing rent-seeking, and adversely influencing legal and economic institutions (Remmer 2004; Rajan and Subramanian 2005, 2007; Heckelman and Knack 2008).

6. Apparently most of the studies on the aid–growth relationship tested a linear relationship using simple OLS methodology.

The second group of studies suggests that *foreign aid in all likelihood positively influences economic growth, but with diminishing returns,* and that its effect is unconditional to the policy environment (Durbarry, Gemmell, and Greenaway 1998; Dalgaard and Hansen 2000; Hansen and Tarp 2000, 2001; Lensink and White 2001; Dalgaard, Hansen, and Tarp 2004; and others).[7] Most of these studies have concluded that although aid has not always worked, on average, higher aid flows have been associated with more rapid growth. For instance, Hansen and Tarp (2000, 2001) formulated an empirical framework to allow for nonlinearities in the aid–growth relationship, such as quadratic aid and policy along with aid policy interactions. They also controlled for some economic, political, and institutional variables. They found that the coefficient for the aid variable is positive and statistically significant, but the coefficient for aid squared is statistically significant and negative. In other words, they showed that the causal relationship between aid and growth is positive but that this positive impact diminishes as the volume of aid increases.

Lensink and White (2001) developed an interesting theoretical model and empirical approach to examine the idea of nonlinearity in the aid–growth relationship. They claimed not only that aid might have diminishing returns but that, after a certain level, returns might become negative. They found that the threshold for negative marginal returns is 50 percent of the ratio of aid to GNP. The significance of this finding might be limited, however, given that 50 percent of the ratio of aid to GNP exceeds the average aid ratio for most aid recipient countries. Some other authors have found that the threshold for negative marginal return to aid is about 25 percent of GDP (Hadjimichael et al. 1995; Hansen and Tarp 2000).

More recently, Arndt, Jones, and Tarp (2010), using an IV approach, reexamined the aid–growth relationship. They modified the instrumentation strategy suggested by Rajan and Subramanian (2008) by dropping the colonizer-specific variables and their interactions with the population ratio and by adding donor-specific fixed effects. Another important modification is that Arndt, Jones, and Tarp (2010) used aid per capita as the dependent variable instead of the ratio of aid to GDP. Then they used the Heckman estimator to construct the complicated instrument for aid. The results obtained in a cross-sectional IV framework suggest that aid has a positive and statistically significant causal effect on growth over the long run. Therefore, they concluded that "aid has been and remains a key tool for enhancing the development prospects of poor nations" (Arndt, Jones, and Tarp 2010, 24).

The third group of studies suggests that *aid has a conditional positive impact on growth,* helping recipients only in certain circumstances. This conditional strand indicates that aid supported growth only in certain circumstances but not in other situations. For example, Guillaumont and Chauvet (2001) found

7. Some suggest that the diminishing returns reflect absorptive capacity constraint, an idea that dates back to the 1950s and 1960s and stems from limits in the quality and quantity of human capital and physical infrastructure (Quibria 2004).

that aid works positively in countries with difficult economic environments, as characterized by unstable terms of trade and natural disasters. The findings of Collier and Dehn (2001) support the results obtained by Guillaumont and Chauvet (2001). Collier and Dehn measured vulnerability by the change in export prices and showed that the interaction term involving the change in aid and the change in export prices is significant.

Another well-publicized and influential study that belongs to the conditional strand is the study by Burnside and Dollar (2000). They applied the empirical strategy of making the impact of aid dependent on a summary measure reflecting the quality of policies instead of vulnerabilities. They defined a "good policy environment" as a weighted combination of low inflation, low budget deficits, and trade openness. Then they introduced aid (as a share of GNP) as well as the interaction of aid and the composite policy variable in a standard growth regression. Their results showed that the coefficient for aid by itself is not significantly different from zero, but the coefficient for the interaction term is positive and statistically significant, implying that aid works in "a good policy environment" but has little impact in "a poor policy environment" (Burnside and Dollar 2000; see also World Bank 1998).

The findings of Burnside and Dollar (2000) have been extremely influential and have decisively changed the debate on aid effectiveness and donors' aid allocation policies. If foreign aid stimulates economic growth in countries with good policies, foreign aid should be given selectively to countries that have adopted sound policies. Multilateral and bilateral donors have recognized the importance of this finding and started to pay more attention to recipients' policies in their aid allocation decisions (World Bank 1998, 2002; DFID 2000; USAID 2002). The findings of Burnside and Dollar (2000) also suggested a specific criterion for targeting aid. This criterion is called a "poverty-efficient allocation of aid" (Collier and Dollar 2002, 1476), and it focuses on those countries with a combination of high rates of poverty and a good policy environment (Collier and Dollar 2002). The basic message of this criterion is that poor countries with good policy environments, as measured by the World Bank Country Policy and Institutional Assessment (CPIA) index, should be eligible for aid, whereas countries with low CPIA scores should not be eligible for aid or, alternatively, receive less aid. This idea has been adopted by the International Development Association and the UK Department for International Development (Dalgaard, Hansen, and Tarp 2004). The Millennium Challenge Corporation of the United States also uses similar methodology to determine the countries eligible for its aid.

However, some researchers have questioned the robustness of the Burnside and Dollar (2000) findings and concluded that there is a need for more research on the subject. First, Hansen and Tarp found that "the basic Burnside-Dollar results turn out to be sensitive to data and model specification" (2000, 125). They argued that by changing the number of observations and the model specification one can make the crucial aid–policy interaction term significant and also turn off this result. More recently Easterly, Levine, and Roodman (2004) reassessed the links among foreign aid, policy, and growth using extended data. Although the Burnside and Dollar (2000) results were based on a panel of 56 countries and six four-year time periods from 1970–73 to 1990–93, Easterly, Levine, and Roodman (2004) extended the number of observations by adding additional countries and one more time period (1994–97). Thus, using the same methodology, their study re-examined whether foreign aid has a positive effect on economic growth in the presence of sound policies. They did not find that foreign aid promotes economic growth in good policy environments. These new findings cast doubt on the previous conclusion that aid will promote growth in countries with good policies. Burnside and Dollar (2004), responding to the critique, argued that the results of the studies by Easterly, Levine, and Roodman (2004) in fact suggest "a positive, though nonlinear, relationship between aid and growth for countries with good policies" (Burnside and Dollar 2004, 783).

All of the studies reviewed earlier have one common characteristic: they examined the impact of aggregate aid on growth.[8] However, not all aid is alike in its impact on growth. Some types of aid (such as aid to the agricultural sector) are more likely to accelerate growth by directly influencing production, while other types are more likely to boost domestic consumption by providing, for example, food aid. Therefore, given the heterogeneity of aid flows based on their likely impact on growth, it is not surprising that the evidence on the relationship between aid and growth is inconclusive. In this regard, one of the increasingly popular directions in the aid–growth literature in recent years has been toward investigating the impact of different categories of aid. Researchers have tried to disaggregate aid in terms of motives for granting aid, donor type, the timing of aid's impact, and the use to which aid is put (Rajan and Subramanian 2008).

Concerning the motives for granting aid, Bourguignon and Sundberg (2007) argue that there should be no prior expectations of positive effects of aid that is given for strategic purposes, because this type of aid is systematically given to countries with bad policies or institutions. Minoiu and Reddy (2009) find that developmental aid provided by the multilateral donors and Scandinavian countries is usually more effective in promoting long-term growth than that given by other bilateral donors. However, Rajan and Subramanian (2008) find no difference between the effects of multilateral and bilateral aid and the effects of aid given by Scandinavian and other donors. Rajan and Subramanian (2008) also find that neither social aid nor economic aid has a significant positive impact on economic growth. However, it is not clear what estimation strategy they used in this analysis or for what covariates they controlled.

8. Rajan and Subramanian (2008) try to distinguish the impact of different types of aid following Clemens, Radelet, and Bhavnan (2004).

The third basis for disaggregating aid is the timing of its impact. In this regard, a study by Clemens, Radelet, and Bhavnani (2004) and Radelet, Clemens, and Bhavnani (2005) focused on the type of aid that is directed primarily at growth and examined the relationship between aid and growth for a sample of 67 countries between 1974 and 2001. They divided aggregate aid into three mutually exclusive, collectively exhaustive categories: "short-impact" aid, "long-impact" aid, and "humanitarian" aid. In their classification, short-impact aid includes aid to build infrastructure and to support productive sectors. Aid that comes in the form of cash to provide support to the budget or balance of payments is also included in this category. Long-impact aid includes aid to social infrastructure and environmental conservation. Humanitarian aid comprises aid for disasters, emergencies, and relief efforts, including food aid. The authors focused on short-impact aid (about 53 percent of all aid flows) and found that this type of aid has a strong, positive, and causal effect on economic growth. The results suggest that an increase of 1 percentage point of GDP in short-impact aid produced an additional 0.31 percentage point of annual growth over the four-year period. The researchers found at the mean that an increase of $1.00 in short-impact aid raises output (and income) by $1.64 in terms of net present value in a typical aid recipient country. This impact is two to three times greater than in studies using aggregate aid. The study also found diminishing returns to aid: the maximum growth rate occurs when short-impact aid reaches 8 percent of a recipient's GDP.

Finally, researchers have disaggregated aid by purpose. Owens and Hoddinott (1999) found that aid to infrastructure and agricultural extension in Zimbabwe increased household welfare far more than did humanitarian (food and emergency) aid. Mavrotas (2003) disaggregated aid to Uganda by program, project, technical assistance, and food aid. He then used a time-series error-correction model to test the growth impact of aid and found that program aid had a much larger positive impact than did project aid. He also found that technical cooperation and food aid had significantly negative impacts. Cordella and Dell'Ariccia (2003) disaggregated development assistance into program and project aid, then found evidence that program aid is preferable for growth than project aid when donors' and recipients' preferences are aligned. These studies were mainly country specific. Mishra and Newhouse (2009) examined the relationship between health aid and infant mortality using panel system GMM regressions. They found that health aid has a beneficial but small effect on infant mortality.

The overview of existing studies on the cross-country relationship between foreign aid and development outcomes, mainly economic growth, provided in this section shows broadly inconclusive and widely divergent results. This exercise provides important methodological and practical insights into how to examine the relationship between aid and growth. In particular, it highlights the importance of disaggregating total aid into subcomponents when studying this relationship.

What Determines Foreign Aid?

There is a broad body of empirical literature that explores this question. The evidence suggests that aid efforts are remarkably fragmented across all dimensions—number of donors giving aid, number of recipients receiving aid from a given donor, and number of sectors in which a given donor operates (Easterly and Pfutze 2008). The past empirical literature in this regard can be categorized in two ways. First, most of this literature has been devoted to examining the observed aid allocation patterns. Second, a small but rapidly growing body of literature has sought to explain the forces that shape aid flows. Recent comprehensive reviews of these studies can be found in Dollar and Levin (2004), McGillivray (2004), and Berthélemy (2006b). This literature suggests that donors seem to be neither entirely altruistic nor completely self-serving; that is, in their aid allocation donors aim to promote their own interests as well as meet the needs of recipient countries. Some stylized facts suggest that several factors are important in determining donors' aid allocation decisions:

- *Recipients' needs.* It appears that promoting economic development and welfare in recipient countries has some importance to most donors making aid allocation decisions. Moreover, for the three decades preceding the War on Terror, there was a clear, steadily increasing trend in the importance of recipients' needs in the allocation of foreign aid, which has sharply reversed since the beginning of War on Terror (Fleck and Kilby 2010). Also, donors seem more concerned with alleviating physical miseries (infant mortality) but less with reducing poverty (Younas 2008).
- *Donors' strategic and political interests.* The literature suggests that some of the variation in aid flows can be explained by donors' strategic assessments of changing international situations (Alesina and Dollar 2000). These political and strategic considerations continue to be the major determinants of aid allocation even in the post–Cold War era (Younas 2008). Donors seem to give a certain amount of aid on the basis of political considerations, even if this is suboptimal from the perspective of poverty reduction (de Mesquita and Smith 2009).
- *Donors' economic (commercial) interests.* Such interests also explain a significant part of the variation in foreign aid flows; that is, donors allocate some aid with the aim of expanding their own markets, creating sources of inexpensive imports from developing countries, and protecting the foreign investments of their private companies. Some recent studies suggest that such commercial interests play a major role and have a much greater quantitative influence on aid allocation than do geopolitical motives (Berthélemy 2006b).
- *Population bias.* Donors seem to think that their aid would have a greater impact in smaller countries due to the decreasing marginal benefits of

aid allocation as population size increases, the relatively smaller aid-absorbing capacity of more populous countries, and so on (Trumbull and Wall 1994; Neumayer 2003).

- *Differences between multilateral and bilateral donors.* Multilateral donors focus more on recipients' needs, whereas bilateral donors pay more attention to their own strategic and economic interests (Maizels and Nissanke 1984).
- *Differences among bilateral donors.* These differences are related to the roles of self-interest and recipient needs in donors' aid allocation policies. Four Nordic countries, including Denmark, Finland, Norway, and Sweden, behave similarly in that they allocate more aid to recipients with less per capita income, open economies, and democratic governance. At the same time, larger donors such as France, Japan, and the United States allocate more aid to their political allies and former colonies at the margin and pay less attention to recipients' needs and good governance (Alesina and Dollar 2000).
- *The "bandwagon effect."* Despite important differences among them, bilateral donors' aid allocation decisions are influenced by the donors' expectations that the impact of their aid on a recipient country would be higher if other donors were to grant greater amounts to a recipient country (Dudley and Montmarquette 1976; Alesina and Dollar 2000).
- *Perceptions of recipients' governance.* The empirical findings regarding the recent rhetoric of donors to the effect that aid rewards efficient and accountable governments by allocating more aid to countries with good performance on the various aspects of good governance are mixed. Some studies have found that most donors increasingly reward good economic policy outcomes and pay greater attention to good governance in recipient countries (Berthélemy and Tichit 2004; Dollar and Levin 2004). Others argue that donors allocate more aid to recipients with better governance only at the margin (Alesina and Dollar 2000; Neumayer 2003). Therefore, a lot of foreign aid still goes to corrupt and autocratic governments (Easterly and Pfutze 2008).

A more detailed review of the aid allocation literature leads to the following observations. Although most recent empirical studies do not explicitly present the theoretical framework embodied in their regressions, it is possible to incorporate them into the theoretical framework proposed by earlier literature (Dudley and Montmarquette 1976; Trumbull and Wall 1994). This earlier literature includes some valuable insights as to the modeling of foreign aid. The framework is based on the standard microeconomic theory of constrained utility maximization and attempts to explain bilateral donors' two decisions: first, whether to give aid to a given developing country (eligibility stage) and, second, how much aid to grant given that a positive decision had been made at the first stage (level stage). It emphasizes the public good aspect of foreign aid from a donor's perspective: in particular, a donor maximizes the relative impact of its aid on the recipient country, as measured by the ratio of the per capita aid to the per capita income, weighed by the size of the recipient's population.

The model's main assumptions are that the donor country may expect that (1) the recipient country will behave more favorably toward the donor country by supporting the donor's national political interests, (2) the recipient country will confer economic benefits on the donor by buying more products from the donor country, and (3) the lives of people in the recipient country will be better because of the donor's assistance (altruistic vision). Although the first two assumptions refer to donors' interests, the third assumption refers to recipients' needs. By solving the utility maximization problem subject to budget constraint, Dudley and Montmarquette (1976) derived two econometric specifications to test the relative importance of various factors in donors' aid allocation decisions. Trumbull and Wall (1994) extended this model to allow optimization by multiple donors, assuming that all donors have the same subjective measure of the impact of aid on a recipient country.

Although existing empirical literature often uses per capita income in recipient countries as an indicator of recipients' needs, other variables such as infant mortality, the literacy rate, and life expectancy are also widely used in aid allocation regressions for that purpose. The following variables are widely used to control for donors' interests: recipients' political connection with donors, donors' military presence in recipients' countries, religious similarity and geographic proximity of donors and recipients, and trade and investment relations between donors and recipients. For example, Alesina and Dollar (2000) controlled for donors' interests (mostly strategic and political interests) using such variables as colonial experience, UN voting similarity, and the share of Muslims and Roman Catholics in the recipients' population and for recipients' needs through per capita income. Another study by Apodaca and Stohl (1999), exploring US foreign aid allocation, found support for recipients' needs at the eligibility stage and for donor interests and human rights at both the eligibility and level stages. The findings of this study suggest that, although the impact of recipients' needs, as measured by per capita GNP, on the aid allocation decisions made by the US government is positive and statistically significant, US national security interests play a more prominent role in aid allocation than recipients' needs. The United States gives aid to countries perceived as vital to US national security, as well as to most Latin American countries, regardless of other factors.

As mentioned earlier, there is another small but growing body of literature that investigates the incentives in donor–recipient relations, the interactions between official and private aid, and the attitudes toward foreign aid in donor countries. Svensson (2000b) uses a game-theoretic model in which an altruistic donor allocates aid according to recipients' needs and the aid allocation rule adversely affects recipients' incentives to carry out policies to improve human development indicators: infant mortality, life expectancy, and primary school enrollment. The empirical tests show that recipients' needs and population are the main determinants of aid allocation, but aid flows have no statistically significant impact on promoting human development indicators. Also, some authors investigated donors' aid allocation policies by examining the interactions between donors and recipients (Svensson 2000a). These studies show how policy differences across donors may affect the development outcomes. They stress the importance of the timing of aid disbursements and the degree to which aid flows are aimed at the poor in terms of outcomes. Another study, focusing on the interaction between official and private aid, found that the provision of official assistance relative to private foreign aid varies significantly between donors and that official aid crowds out private aid (Schweinberger and Lahiri 2006).

In the wake of the latest political developments and changes in development thinking, recently donor countries have started to reconsider their aid allocation policies by focusing on the quality of governance in the recipient countries. Some important research has examined the efficiency of aid allocation in this regard. The literature uses various indicators to measure the quality of governance in recipient countries, including personal integrity rights (Apodaca and Stohl 1999), political rights and civil liberties (Trumbull and Wall 1994; Alesina and Dollar 2000; Neumayer 2003), and the rule of law and corruption (Alesina and Weder 1999; Alesina and Dollar 2000; Neumayer 2003). In particular, Alesina and Weder (1999) investigate the impact of the level of corruption in the recipient country on aid flows and find no evidence that corruption negatively affects the amount of overall foreign aid flows. However, the Scandinavian countries appear to reward less corrupt countries with greater amounts of aid, and large donors such as Japan, the United Kingdom, and the United States appear to be indifferent to the level of corruption in a recipient country. According to Neumayer (2003), all aspects of good governance (he controls for democracy, human rights, corruption, rule of law, and regulatory burden) except for the rule of law have statistically significant effects on donors' decisions at the eligibility stage. He also finds that democracy, respect for human rights, and a low level of regulatory burden are statistically significant determinants of aid flows for some donors. Alesina and Dollar (2000) also find that, at the margin, developing countries that support political rights and civil liberties receive more aid, ceteris paribus. Chong and Gradstein (2008) suggest that political support for foreign aid in donor countries is mainly affected by their own governments' efficiency and less by that of recipient countries.

The literature also examines the relationship between foreign aid and the quality of governance in recipient countries. Knack (2000) examines the interdependence between foreign aid and the quality of governance by relating the quality of governance to foreign aid, measured as a percentage of GDP and a percentage of government expenditures. The quality of governance is measured by the International Country Risk Guide (ICRG) indexes of bureaucratic quality, the rule of law, and corruption. The paper finds that higher levels of foreign aid erode the quality of governance. Similarly, Knack and Rahman (2007) provide theoretical analysis and empirical evidence of the impact of donor fragmentation on the quality of government bureaucracy in aid recipient countries. Their results suggest that competitive donor practices and fragmentation erode administrative capacity and bureaucratic quality in recipient countries' governments.

The review of these studies also shows that the econometrics of aid allocation has evolved over time by addressing some specific characteristics of aid allocation. Evidence shows that some individual donors provide a positive amount of aid to some recipients and nothing to others: larger donors (France, Germany, Japan, the United Kingdom, and the United States) tend to give some amount of aid to most recipients, while smaller donors (such as Denmark, Finland, and Ireland) tend to focus on fewer recipients. This makes the dependent variable censored, given that it cannot be negative and can be only partly continuous, with a positive probability mass at the value of zero. This creates a problem for standard linear regression models because they depend on the assumption that the expected value of the dependent variable is linear relative to the exploratory variables. Therefore, aid allocation literature uses limited-dependent variable methods: a two-part model (Apodaca and Stohl 1999; Neumayer 2003; and others), Heckman's two-step procedure (Trumbull and Wall 1994; Berthélemy 2006a; and others), or Tobit regressions (Alesina and Weder 1999; Alesina and Dollar 2000). More recently, Berthélemy and Tichit (2004) and Berthélemy (2006a, 2006b) have further polished the econometric methodology used in aid allocation analysis by allowing for both sample selection and time-invariant unobservable heterogeneity. Although they used more advanced techniques, their results broadly support the findings of earlier studies.

Governance and Its Relation to Growth

Overall, successful long-term development is a complex process that depends on many factors. Nevertheless, the evidence suggests that the quality of governance in a country is particularly important and heavily influences its development. Compared to this factor, other factors including foreign aid appear to be much less important in determining whether a given country will achieve its development objectives, such as long-term economic growth and poverty reduction. Foreign aid is likely to be most helpful when it is combined with better governance. However, what do we understand by the quality of governance? What is the evidence regarding the role of governance in economic development? In order to answer these questions, this section briefly reviews the definitions and indicators of governance, then discusses its relation to economic development and the effectiveness of foreign aid.

The quality of governance in developing countries has recently moved into the spotlight of the development debate. Several factors have contributed to the growing interest in the quality of governance: (1) the end of the Cold War; (2) the failure of structural adjustment reforms in many developing countries in the 1980s and 1990s; (3) the problems associated with reforming the transition economies of Eastern Europe and the former Soviet Union; (4) the impressive growth of international capital flows, especially foreign direct investment; and (5) a new awareness of the importance of institutions (political and economic) and politics in economic development and progress (Feng 2004; Wolfenson and Bourguignon 2004; Arndt and Oman 2006). Additional interest in the quality of governance is being generated by donors' increasing focus on performance-based aid allocation policies.

Despite the growing popularity of governance at both the theoretical and policy levels, the term continues to mean different things to different people. Some focus on outcomes—the extent to which governments enact and implement policies in the interest of all citizens. Others concentrate on institutions and processes that determine these outcomes—the extent to which governments have incentives to embrace and enforce policies in the interest of all people. For example, the *Oxford English Dictionary* (OED 2011) defines *governance* as "the action or manner of governing; controlling, directing, or regulating influence; . . . method of management, system of regulations." The United Nations Development Programme (UNDP) has adopted a definition of governance as "the exercise of economic, political, and administrative authority to manage a country's affairs at all levels" (UNDP 1997, 2–3). Based on this definition, governance involves the mechanisms, processes, and institutions through which citizens and government institutions exercise their legal rights, meet their obligations, and mediate conflicts. In this context, three dimensions of governance are identified: political, economic, and administrative. The political dimension comprises policy formulation, the economic dimension includes the decisionmaking process that affects a country's domestic economic activities and its relationship with the international economy, and the administrative dimension involves the system of policy implementation. In an influential study, Kaufmann, Kraay, and Zoido-Lobaton (1999) suggested a broad and comprehensive view of governance that defines it as the combination of rules and institutions by which a country is governed. This view includes three dimensions of governance: (1) the way governments are selected, monitored, and replaced; (2) the capacity of the government to effectively formulate and implement policies; and (3) the respect of citizens and the state for the rules and institutions that govern political, social, and economic interactions among them (Kaufmann, Kraay, and Zoido-Lobaton 1999).

The definitional ambiguity surrounding the term *governance* is particularly challenging when trying to measure the quality of governance. Nevertheless, in response to growing interest in the quality of governance, the supply of governance indicators has grown significantly in recent years. Considered the most comprehensive measurement of the quality of governance, aggregate governance indicators developed by Kaufmann, Kraay, and Zoido- Lobaton (1999) combine various measures of governance into six composite indicators corresponding to three dimensions of governance: (1) voice and accountability refers to whether citizens participate in the selection and monitoring of their governments; (2) political stability measures whether the government is vulnerable to change through violence; (3) government effectiveness examines the capacity of civil servants, the quality of public service provision, and the credibility of government commitment to policies; (4) regulatory quality indicates whether the policies promoted are "market friendly" in the areas of trade and business; (5) rule of law focuses on the enforcement of property rights and the predictability of rules governing social and economic interactions; and (6) control of corruption refers to whether there is evidence of the "exercise of public power for private gain" (Kaufmann, Kraay, and Zoido-Lobaton 1999, 8). These six indicators are composite in the sense that they were constructed, using the unobserved components method, from more than 200 existing measures of governance from 37 different databases. Although these aggregate indicators of governance are widely acknowledged and used by academia and the development community, some caution that the methodology used and the changing composition of the indicators over time makes them unreliable to use in comparing levels of governance over time, be it in a single country or between countries (Arndt and Oman 2006). Glaeser et al. (2004) argued that these indicators measure outcomes, not permanent characteristics of governance institutions that tend to improve with per capita income.

A second important source of governance indicators is Freedom House, whose annual ratings of political rights and civil liberties are widely used to measure the strengths of democratic governance in more than 190 countries worldwide. The political rights index intends to capture the extent to which citizens can participate in the political process by competing for public office and exercising a right to vote. The civil liberties index aims to measure whether citizens have sufficient freedom to develop opinions and personal autonomy without state interference. Another commonly used governance indicator is the previously mentioned ICRG rating system, which is produced by the Political Risk Services Group. The ICRG system is based on "a set of 22 components grouped into three major categories of risk: political, financial, and economic risk" (PRS Group Inc. 2011, 2). The financial and economic risk assessments are based entirely on objective data, such as a country's foreign debt and debt service ratio, international liquidity, current account and budget deficits, growth rates, inflation, and so on. In contrast, the political risk assessments rely on subjective expert assessments of the prespecified risk components. The country ratings are designed to be comparable over time and across countries.

A brief look at some widely used definitions and indicators of governance shows that all definitions and indicators relate governance to institutions. This is plausible because institutions craft order and reshape incentives, thus building the governance structure of a country and leading to the formation of national government (Jütting 2003). It is also evident that governance indicators capture two sides of governance: political or democratic governance and economic governance. Democratic governance refers to political institutions such as political rights, civil liberties, and political stability. In contrast, economic governance refers to the legal and social institutions that support economic activity by protecting property rights, enforcing contracts, and promoting collective action to provide physical and organizational infrastructure (Dixit 2009).

The existing literature has developed various arguments that link democratic and economic governance. On the one side, by definition, democracies tend to make the quality of (economic) governance better in the long run by allowing people to peacefully and regularly get rid of incompetent and inefficient governments while allowing them to keep competent and efficient governments. On the other side, nondemocratic regimes can sometimes provide highly efficient and competent governments, as in China, Malaysia, Singapore, and South Korea (in the 1980s). However, if nondemocratic regimes do not provide efficient and competent government, people cannot easily and peacefully get rid of them. Overall, the evidence suggests that stronger democratic institutions are closely associated with better quality of governance (Rivera-Batiz 2002).

There is broad agreement that the quality of governance significantly affects economic outcomes. However, there are serious disputes about details of the causal mechanisms by which governance affects economic outcomes. The literature shows that various governance indicators are positively correlated with measures of per capita income across countries. However, the findings concerning the direction of causality between the quality of governance and the level of per capita income in a country are not conclusive. The results are very sensitive to changes in econometric model specifications and the variables included in the model (Arndt and Oman 2006). For example, Kaufmann and Kraay (2002), in a cross-country study, conclude that although better governance tends to clearly promote growth in per capita income, growth in per capita income per se does not tend to promote better governance. In a similar study, Rodrik, Subramanian, and Trebbi (2004) find that the observed direct effect of the institutional quality of governance on per capita income is positive and both statistically and practically significant.[9] However, Arndt and Oman (2006), using the same measures of governance, find that the relationship between the quality of governance and per capita income is complicated. Their findings suggest that per capita income tends to have a positive impact on governance and vice versa. They conclude that the direction of causality might be

9. Rodrik, Subramanian, and Trebbi (2004) use the Rule of Law indicator from Kaufmann, Kraay, and Zoido-Lobaton (2003) to measure the institutional quality of governance.

different for different groups of countries or there may be different stages of relationship between governance and per capita income.

Several studies use the ICRG indicators of governance or IVs for institutions to establish the causality between institutions, which are at the core of governance. Hall and Jones (1999), using equally weighed averages of five indicators from the ICRG (law and order, bureaucratic quality, corruption, risk of expropriation, and government repudiation of contracts), find that the differences in capital accumulation, productivity, and thus output per worker are driven by differences in institutions and government policies. Acemoglu, Johnson, and Robinson (2001) argue that Europeans adopted very different colonization policies in different colonies, with different associated institutions: in places where they faced high mortality rates, these colonizers could not settle permanently, and they were thus more likely to establish extractive institutions, which persisted after independence; in places where they could settle permanently, they established more development-minded institutions. Thus, by using differences in European mortality rates as an instrument for institutions, Acemoglu, Johnson, and Robinson (2001) find large effects of institutions on per capita income.

Further, a number of authors examine the connection between democratic governance and economic outcomes. Democracy can be important for economic development because its reliance on rules and procedures provides citizens with protection against predation by government bureaucrats. That is why establishing democratic institutions and other checks on government as the mechanisms for securing property rights seems very important. With such democratic institutions in place, investment in human and physical capital, and therefore economic growth, are expected to follow. But even in a democracy, various agents may pursue their private interests using rent-seeking and corruption. Emerging literature argues that economic development, at least in the early stages, is better promoted under suitable authoritarian regimes. For example, Glaeser et al. (2004) argue that less developed countries that achieve economic development do so by pursuing good economic policies, often under autocracies. This assumes that even pro-market autocratic regimes can secure property rights as a matter of policy choice, not of political constraints, and this allows human and physical capital accumulation to start the process. This approach sees democracy and other improvements in governance as the consequences of increased education and wealth (Glaeser et al. 2004).

Przeworski et al. (2000), using transparent data for more than 140 countries from between 1950 and 1990, find that although democracies and nondemocracies grow on average at similar rates, nondemocracies tend to have higher population growth rates, which means that per capita growth rates tend to be lower in nondemocracies. They also find that per capita income growth has a significant positive impact on the probability of a country's making the transition to democracy and vice versa. Their findings further indicate that per capita income growth has a significant stabilizing effect on democracies. Empirical evidence presented by Rivera-Batiz (2002) suggests that democracy is a significant determinant of total factor productivity growth in a cross section of countries. However, the article also indicates that democracy makes a positive contribution to growth only to the extent that stronger democratic institutions are associated with better-quality overall governance. Likewise, democracy plays a crucial role in sustaining long-term growth when it accompanies strong market institutions, but without strong market institutions democracy is not able to sustain growth (Bhagwati 1995). In contrast, the experiences of China and other newly industrialized countries of East Asia show that even nondemocratic governments with strong markets and public policies can facilitate and sustain long-term economic growth (World Bank 1993).

Besides providing evidence of the direct impact of governance on development outcomes, the literature suggests that governance and institutions have an indirect impact on economic growth and development. This indirect effect appears to run through their impact on investment, conflict prevention and mitigation, policies, and the stock of social capital (Jütting 2003). In this context, Fedderke, Klitgaard, and Akramov (2005) find that governance has an indirect as well as a direct impact on output. They estimate that the productivity of investment increases by a factor of 1.6 between countries with the worst governance and those with moderate governance. The indirect impact of governance on development outcomes might have important implications for the effectiveness of aid. The challenge for research is to identify the potential effects of interaction between governance and foreign aid.

In fact, an emerging literature examines the potential interaction effects of governance and foreign aid on economic outcomes. Svensson (2000a) finds that foreign aid may be positively associated with economic growth in democracies but detrimental in nondemocratic aid recipient (developing) countries. Kosack (2003) finds that aid is effective in democracies in its ability to improve the quality of life proxied by the UNDP Human Development Index but ineffective in autocracies. The reason for this outcome is that democracies are inclined toward the immediate demands of citizens, unlike autocracies. Hodler (2007) likewise suggests that the rent-seeking behavior of elites is an important factor in explaining the effectiveness of aid. Therefore, the absence of democratic checks and balances on politicians and elites is often implicitly blamed for the absence of beneficial effects from foreign aid in promoting economic growth. However, in a more recent paper Bjórnskov (2010) finds that foreign aid leads to a more skewed income distribution in democratic developing countries, while the effects are negligible in autocratic countries.

As indicated in the introduction, the main objective of this study is to examine how foreign aid is allocated, how such allocation takes into account the quality of recipients' governance, and how current allocation patterns might have affected the effectiveness of aid, that is, by promoting development outcomes in recipient countries. In reality, as suggested by previous studies, multiple factors influence donors' aid allocation decisions and the effectiveness of aid. In order to improve the effectiveness of foreign aid, donors' aid allocation decisions should be guided by evidence-based results. Nevertheless, previous research on the topic has rarely linked the effectiveness of ODA to foreign aid allocation patterns. Studies aiming to explain determinants of aid flows do not consider effectiveness issues and vice versa. This study addresses this weakness of the literature by linking sectoral aid allocation patterns and the effectiveness of aid through recipients' quality of governance. There are complex interactions between governance and growth outside of foreign aid. Although I try to control for these factors in the empirical analysis, my main focus is on the interaction of governance and aid flows.

Concerning the impact of aid on development, two contrasting experiences are possible within which individual national practice may lie. At one extreme, foreign aid may contribute to a virtuous circle of development by initiating required institutional and policy changes, relaxing savings and foreign exchange constraints, and easing the access to international capital markets. The experiences of several Asian countries, such as the Republic of Korea, Taiwan, and some others, appear to lie close to this extreme. These countries benefited from extensive foreign assistance in earlier years, which allowed them to develop their economies and build democratic governance. At the other extreme, foreign assistance may contribute to a vicious circle by delaying necessary institutional and policy reforms and encouraging rent-seeking behavior and corruption both within society and inside government structures. The experiences of many countries in Sub-Saharan Africa appear to lie close to this extreme (Mavrotas 2003).

Given this discussion, it is appropriate to hypothesize an important role for the quality of governance in analyses of the effectiveness and allocation of aid. A focus on governance should not imply that the variables emphasized by previous studies are unimportant, but it does lead to a different emphasis in empirical inquiries. In this study, my proposition is that differences in the quality of governance and their interactions with different categories of aid flows play an indispensable role in improving the effectiveness of foreign aid in promoting development outcomes. If differences in governance and its interaction with different categories of foreign aid often decisively influenced the effectiveness of aid, lack of control for these interactions would plausibly lead to biased and inconsistent results regarding the effectiveness of aid. By explicitly incorporating interactions of governance with different categories of aid into the model, this research aims to mitigate this problem. This will allow us to evaluate the role of governance in improving the impact of aid in order to answer critical policy questions such as those on the allocation of aid not only between recipient countries but also across different sectors of their economies.

3 Data and Descriptive Analysis

This chapter describes data sources, measurement issues, and descriptive analysis of data. A panel dataset covering aid from both bilateral and multilateral donors over the past five decades was compiled for the purposes of empirical analysis (see Appendix B for a list of donors and recipient countries). I use data from various sources. First, the study relies heavily on data from OECD's Development Assistance Committee (DAC) database (OECD, Development Database on Aid from DAC Members: DAC Online, various years), as well as from its Credit Reporting System (CRS) (OECD, Development Database on Aid Activities: CRS Online, various years). The OECD databases cover bilateral and multilateral donors' ODA to developing countries. The DAC annual aggregates database provides comprehensive data on the volume, origin, and types of development assistance. The CRS aid activities database provides detailed information on individual aid activities, such as sectors of destination, countries, and project descriptions. As mentioned earlier, according to DAC's definition, foreign aid includes concessional transfers (with a grant element of at least 25 percent) to developing countries from official donor agencies that primarily intend to promote welfare and economic development (which rules out both military and export credits).

Second, I derive data on per capita income, investment, schooling, population, inflation, trade openness, spending on education, and other general socioeconomic variables from different sources, including the Penn World Tables Version 6.3 (Heston, Summers, and Aten 2009) and the World Bank's World Development Indicators database (World Bank 2010). Third, data on exports from donors to recipients are taken from the Direction of Trade Statistics database of the International Monetary Fund (IMF 2006). Fourth, data on governance indicators are taken from Freedom House's Freedom in the World database (Freedom House 2009), the World Bank Institute's Governance database, and the Polity IV database (Marshall, Jaggers, and Gurr 2010). Fifth, data on political similarities are based on the updated version of the Affinity of Nations index (Gartzke 2010) first introduced by Gartzke (1998). The study also uses data on average years of schooling from the Barro and Lee (2003) dataset. Definitions and sources of the variables used in the study are provided in Appendix C.

Disaggregating Aid by Sectors

As mentioned earlier, past research on aid allocation and effectiveness has focused mainly on aggregate aid flows in an attempt to match aid flows to a realistic time period over which they might influence economic growth and other development outcomes.[1] However, as OECD's DAC suggests, aid flows are allocated to different sectors depending on which specific section of a recipient's socioeconomic structure the transfer is intended to promote (OECD 2007). Although one category of contributions might be intended to promote education, another category might be intended to foster agricultural development, and a third category might just be aimed at providing emergency relief. Therefore, these different categories of aid flows are less likely to influence economic growth in the same way and uniformly. Also, it is plausible to expect that the interactions of different categories of aid with various levels of governance in recipient countries will produce different results.

One category of aid might help to foster economic development in a recipient country by building physical capital, while another type of aid might harm incentive structures and encourage rent-seeking behavior. Moreover, aid covers a multitude of different types of transfers, not all of which go directly to recipient countries. Administrative overheads of development agencies and their domestic efforts to advocate in favor of more aid are also counted in aggregate aid flows. Debt forgiveness on nonconcessional loans, which is in reality a flow directly from one branch of government to another agency in a donor country, is also included in development aid. Therefore, any evaluation of the effectiveness of aid when trying to estimate the impact of aggregate aid flows on economic growth and other development outcomes is flawed. However, one can mitigate this challenge to the degree that one can disaggregate aid flows and isolate the impacts of these disaggregated aid flows on development outcomes. Therefore, in contrast to most previous research and in the spirit of Clemens, Radelet, and Bhavnani (2004), I disaggregate aggregate aid into four categories and link the allocation and effectiveness of sectoral aid flows to the recipients' governance. However, unlike Clemens, Radelet, and Bhavnani (2004), I disaggregate aggregate aid flows based on which specific sectors of a recipient's economy transfers are intended to promote.

In disaggregating aid flows by sector, I follow the standard OECD classification. The three mutually exclusive, collectively exhaustive aid categories considered in this study include the following:

1. As we discussed in previous chapters, only a few studies attempted to disaggregate aid flows.

- Economic aid, which in turn can be disaggregated into two subcategories:
  - Aid to the production sectors, which is defined as aid that provides funding for projects in the agriculture, manufacturing, mining, construction, trade, and tourism industries. This aid should plausibly help recipient countries to accumulate physical capital.
  - Aid to economic infrastructure, which is defined as aid intended to build networks and services that facilitate economic activity. This type of aid goes to energy distribution, auto and railroad construction, equipment for communication and electronic networks, and financial infrastructure. This type of aid can probably promote economic growth in recipient countries by improving their overall economic efficiency, boosting their demand for investment, and directly adding to their domestic investment.
- Aid to the social sector, including education, health, and water supply. This aid is more likely to help recipients to build their human capital.
- The remaining aid flows, which are categorized as other aid. This includes aid that provides assistance for the environment, gender projects, food aid, action relating to debt, budget and balance-of-payments support, emergency and distress relief, aid for refugees, and so on. These types of aid have no preimposed sectoral allocation and are intended to smooth short-term fluctuations or to support some longer-term activities rather than to promote economic growth.

The CRS aid activities database provides a set of readily available basic data on sectoral allocation of aid commitments.[2] Data on the amounts of aid disbursements each year are available at the activity level for some donors but not all. The sectoral allocation of aid disbursements must therefore be estimated based on commitments data. To estimate the sectoral allocation of aid disbursements, in this study I use the approach suggested by Clemens, Radelet, and Bhavnani (2004). I classify all (more than 375,000) donor–recipient transactions in the CRS aid activities database from 1973 through 2002 into four sectors, as described earlier. Then I assume that the fraction of aid disbursements in each of the aid categories in a given period was equal to the fraction of commitments in each category in that period.

In reality, there could have been some variations from this equality if there was a time gap between commitments and disbursements. The longer the delay between commitments and disbursements, the greater the variation from the earlier assumption of equality. Clemens, Radelet, and Bhavnani (2004) found that this estimation method is reliable and allows one to estimate disaggregated

2. For most types of aid flows, the CRS Aid Activity database records the face value of the activity on the date that a grant or loan agreement is signed with the recipient. This is called a commitment. The implementation of an aid activity and actual disbursement of aid can go on for several years.

disbursements with a reasonable amount of accuracy, except in the case of humanitarian aid. Further, averaging variables over five-year periods significantly smoothes the short-term fluctuations between commitments and disbursements and reduces the measurement error. The empirical analysis of aid allocation is based on aid commitments, whereas the analysis of aid effectiveness is based on aid disbursements. Although the explanatory analysis that describes the patterns of aid flows covers the latest available data, the econometric analysis (which is presented in the next chapter) covers the aid flows between 1973 and 2002.[3]

Patterns of Foreign Aid Flows

Trends in Aggregate Aid

Figure 3.1 shows trends in aid flows since 1960 as reported by the DAC. Two indicators in constant 2007 prices and exchange rates are shown: aggregate net ODA and weighted average per capita net ODA flows. Total aid flows from all donors have grown, from $36.3 billion in 1960 to almost $114.0 billion in 2008, a multiple of 3.1 times, for an average compound growth of 2.4 percent per year. Of this aggregate, bilateral foreign aid accounts for about 70 percent, while multilateral aid accounts for the remainder. The share of multilateral ODA has remained relatively stable, at 30 percent of total aid flows since the mid-1970s, with the exception of the late 1970s, when multilateral ODA reached 35–36 percent of the total aid flows, and 2005, when its share dropped to 23 percent (Figure 3.2). Among multilateral donor agencies, the most important three aid delivery channels are the European Commission (EC), the United Nations, and the World Bank's International Development Association (IDA). Interestingly, IDA's role as the main channel for delivery of multilateral ODA was surpassed by the EC and the UN agencies in the 1990s (IDA 2007).

Three distinct periods can be seen in trends of aid flows. Overall, as is evident in Figure 3.2, the trends in total aid were largely driven by bilateral flows. This pattern is consistent with the notion that donors' political and economic interests are important determinants of aid. Total aid grew steadily from the 1960s to the early 1990s. However, during this period per capita aid (the weighted mean of per capita averages across aid recipient countries) initially dropped through the early 1970s and then grew steadily following total aid flows.

From 1992 to 1997, aggregate aid dropped by almost 22 percent, which was mainly driven by a dramatic decline in bilateral aid flows. Per capita aid flows also followed the trend in total aid flows. The trend in donor effort, measured as ODA's share of donors' gross national income (GNI), also shows the

3. The reason for limiting the time period in econometric analysis is that DAC provides the CRS data starting from 1973, and the data for 2007 have not been finalized yet to create an additional time period in the panel covering 2003–07.

FIGURE 3.1 Net official development assistance (ODA), 1960–2008 (constant 2007 US dollars)

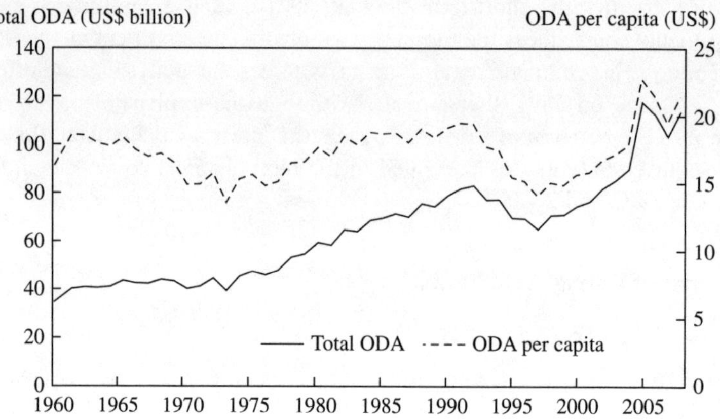

SOURCE: OECD, Development Database on Aid from DAC Members: DAC Online (various years).

FIGURE 3.2 Breakdown of total official development assistance (ODA) by donor type, 1960–2008 (constant 2007 US dollars)

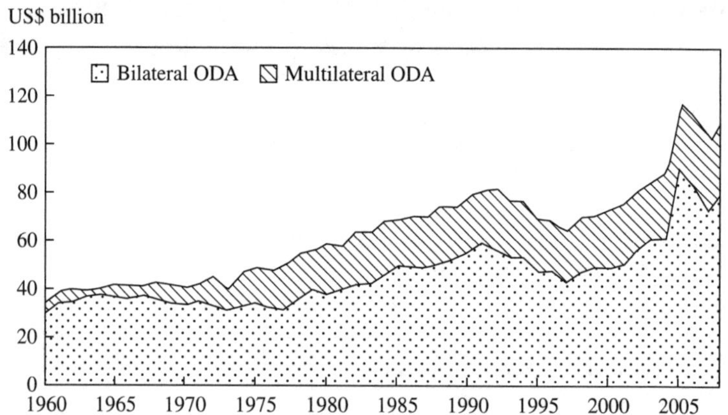

SOURCE: OECD, Development Database on Aid from DAC Members: DAC Online (various years).

deterioration in this period. The average donor effort fluctuated between 0.3 percent and 0.36 percent through the 1970s and 1980s but then fell to 0.22 percent in 1997. This dramatic turnaround in aid flows followed the end of the Cold War. The end of the Cold War dramatically changed the geopolitical picture of the world, and most donors experienced a decline in their aid budgets. The literature provides two plausible explanations in this regard. First, White (2004) argues that the United States has always been the most politically motivated of countries in terms of granting aid, and consequently it lost interest in providing aid with the decline of the Soviet bloc. As a result, the United States' aid effort dropped significantly, from 0.21 percent in 1991 to 0.08 percent in 1997. Second, the drop in aid has been a common phenomenon, one not restricted to the United States. Overall, 16 donors recorded a considerable decline in aid effort. Several European donors that have been running large fiscal deficits, such as Finland, Italy, and Sweden, decreased their aid budgets significantly. Only 4 donors improved their aid effort in this period. The largest improvement in aid effort in this period was that of Japan, which became the largest single donor in the early 1990s, accounting for just over 20 percent of total bilateral aid (White 2004). Some argue that a dramatic decline in official aid inflows to developing countries was compensated with a strong expansion in private capital inflows, including both equity and nonequity flows (Akyuz and Cornford 1999). However, allocation of private capital inflows was skewed toward the emerging markets.

Some important political events around the turn of the millennium have significantly changed donors' perspective toward foreign aid. Since then, actual aid flows have been growing steadily, responding to increasing donor awareness and commitment to problems of developing countries. As shown in Figure 3.1, net ODA disbursements have consistently (with the exception of 2007) risen in real terms since the late 1990s, and they reached $114 billion (at constant 2007 prices) in 2008, up about 75 percent from the amount in 1997. In addition, the recent growth in aid flows has been accompanied by increasingly concessional assistance terms. However, the bulk of this increase in aid flows has been due to debt relief, emergency assistance, and the administrative costs of donors. Aid for core development programs has not grown as fast as total aid flows (IDA 2007).

In this period, the United States regained its position as the world's largest aid donor in terms of ODA volume ($25.4 billion in 2008 at constant 2007 prices), while Japan ($8.3 billion) lost its leading role. At the same time, aid flows from the European Union member countries continued to steadily increase (Figure 3.3). Among the EU members, in terms of aid volume, Germany ($13.0 billion in 2008 at constant 2008 prices), the United Kingdom ($12.2 billion), France ($10.2 billion), and the Netherlands ($6.5 billion) have been the largest bilateral donors. However, in terms of donor aid effort, Sweden (0.98 percent in 2008), Luxembourg (0.92 percent), Norway (0.88 percent), Denmark (0.82 percent), and the Netherlands (0.80 percent) have been the most aid-giving countries. Overall, aid effort has varied quite substantially among the bilateral donors, from 0.18 percent (in Japan and the United States) to 0.98 percent (in Sweden), with a weighted average of 0.30 percent for all DAC members. A closer look at donor aid effort shows that although overall donor effort is considerably greater now than in the 1990s, it is still significantly less than it was in the 1970s.

FIGURE 3.3 Breakdown of total official development assistance by donor, 1960–2008 (constant 2007 US dollars)

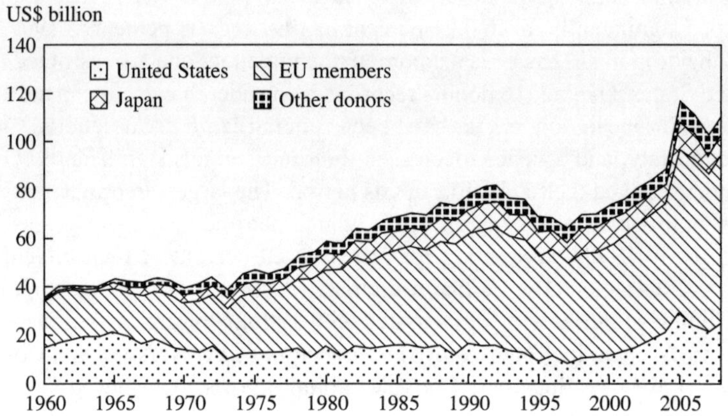

SOURCE: OECD, Development Database on Aid from DAC Members: DAC Online (various years).

Trends in Aid Allocation

This section provides a descriptive overview of aid allocation, identifying which regions and countries received aid and to which sectors of the economy aid was given. Figure 3.4 shows the regional allocation of total aid. It is evident that the share of total aid given to Sub-Saharan Africa (SSA) has increased significantly over time. The countries of the region receive roughly one-third of total ODA, up from less than one-fifth in the early 1970s. Another important development is that the share of total ODA given to Asia has declined from about 40 percent in the early 1970s to less than 20 percent in recent years. This can be partly explained by the successful development efforts of a number of countries in the region, such as China, the Republic of Korea, Malaysia, and Singapore. However, some argue that Asian countries receive less foreign aid in terms of the size of the region's population, the level of income, and the number of poor living there. According to a report of the United Nations Economic and Social Commission for Asia and the Pacific (UNESCAP), per capita aid inflows to SSA, the Commonwealth of Independent States countries of Asia, Western Asia, and the Caribbean range from $21 to $26, while those to South and Southeast Asia range from $10 to $11 per capita (UNESCAP 2006). The report also claims that the share of GNI given as ODA is substantial for SSA in contrast to Asian countries, for example, China and India (0.1 percent and 0.2 percent, respectively). However, the high priority given to SSA by donors can be easily understood in the context of the deep-seated political, social, and economic problems that many countries in the region have been experiencing during the past four decades or so.

FIGURE 3.4 Regional allocation of net official development assistance, 1970–2007

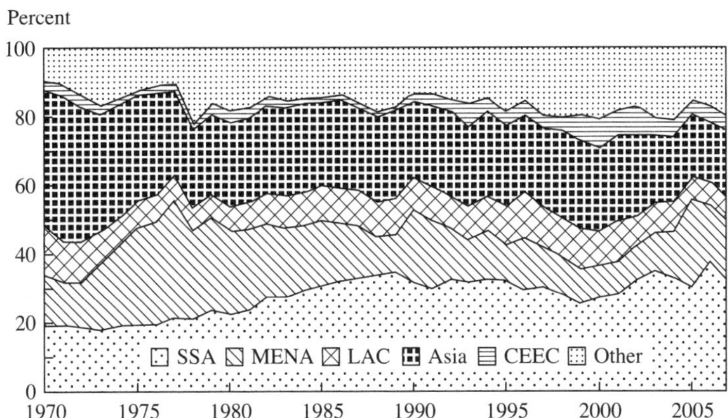

SOURCE: OECD, Development Database on Aid from DAC Members: DAC Online (various years).
NOTES: SSA: Sub-Saharan Africa; MENA: Middle East and North Africa; LAC: Latin America and the Caribbean; CEEC: Central and Eastern European Countries.

Another noteworthy pattern is that although the countries of SSA continue to be major recipients of ODA (in terms of total volumes and per capita aid), in the 1990s countries of Eastern Europe and the former Soviet Union emerged as other favored destinations of foreign aid. Transition countries in this region received on average more than 13 percent of total ODA flows beginning in the early 1990s. On average, countries of this region received about $22 in aid per capita in 2000–04.

In terms of individual-country destinations, there have been notable shifts in the preferences of donors over the past three decades (Table 3.1). First, seven countries of the Asia-Pacific region and two countries of the Middle East and North Africa region together with Turkey were among the 10 largest aid recipients in absolute terms in the early 1970s. However, after three decades only India, Pakistan, and Vietnam were still among the top 10 aid recipients. The other countries were replaced by China, Serbia and Montenegro, Tanzania, Iraq, Mozambique, Russia, and Ethiopia (listed in order of amount of aid). Second, one might ask about per capita aid flows. Table 3.1 shows that only Jordan, among the top 10 per capita aid recipients in 1970–74, remained in the top 10 by 2000–04, while the rest were replaced by other countries. Interestingly, three transition countries (all of them former Yugoslav republics) appeared among the top 10 per capita aid recipients. Another important fact is that the spread of per capita aid inflows among the top 10 aid recipients in terms of both total inflows and per capita aid has become smaller in recent years.

Third, in terms of aid dependence, that is, aid inflows measured as a percentage of recipients' GNI, there have been astonishing changes in most coun-

TABLE 3.1 Top 10 aid recipient developing countries, 1970–74 and 2000–04

Recipient	1970–74	Recipient	2000–04
Average annual net ODA/OA inflows (constant 2003 US dollars)			
India	3,640.3	Congo, Democratic Republic of	1,796.9
Indonesia	2,943.1	Vietnam	1,659.0
Vietnam	1,874.3	China	1,599.0
Egypt	1,804.0	Serbia and Montenegro	1,536.3
Pakistan	1,526.0	Pakistan	1,532.0
Korea Republic	1,354.9	Tanzania	1,485.7
Bangladesh	1,050.3	Iraq	1,428.5
Syria	692.6	Mozambique	1,396.2
Turkey	611.3	Russia	1,386.7
Papua New Guinea	609.6	Ethiopia	1,374.4
Average annual net ODA/OA inflows per capita (constant 2003 million US dollars)			
Suriname	417.9	Micronesia	1,041.8
Djibouti	377.7	Cape Verde	248.9
Solomon Islands	328.6	Tonga	226.5
Jordan	315.9	Serbia and Montenegro	188.9
Belize	257.4	Bosnia and Herzegovina	180.2
Papua New Guinea	228.5	Nicaragua	168.7
Gabon	221.5	Solomon Islands	164.4
Botswana	138.5	Guyana	141.9
Equatorial Guinea	117.6	Macedonia (FYROM)	141.4
Oman	103.3	Jordan	133.6
Net ODA/OA inflows (percentage of gross national income)			
Comoros	36.0	Micronesia	47.0
Solomon Islands	32.4	Guinea-Bissau	38.9
Papua New Guinea	20.8	Sierra Leone	35.9
Cambodia	18.6	Eritrea	35.5
Jordan	15.1	Congo, Democratic Republic of	32.1
Botswana	14.7	Burundi	31.2
Rwanda	12.4	Mozambique	30.5
Lesotho	11.8	Afghanistan	30.4
Suriname	11.6	Solomon Islands	26.2
Mali	11.2	Malawi	25.2

SOURCE: OECD, Development Database on Aid from DAC Members: DAC Online (various years).

NOTES: FYROM: Former Yugoslav Republic of Macedonia; OA: official assistance; ODA: official development assistance.

tries of the SSA region during the past three to four decades. Most countries in this region have experienced a surge in net aid over time, ranging from an average of 5.6 percent of GDP in 1973 to an average of 12.6 percent of GDP in 2002. Today, the level of aid dependence is very high in many SSA countries. Therefore, 7 countries of this region are unsurprisingly among the top 10 aid-dependent countries of the world.

Table 3.2 shows the allocation of aid flows by four income groups: low-income countries; lower-middle-income countries; upper-middle-income countries; and more advanced developing countries and territories. It also shows aid flows that were unallocated by income groups. The notable conclusion we can draw from this table is that the average share of total aid allocated to low-income countries has been greater than 40 percent since the 1970s and reached 46 percent between 2001 and 2007.

However, there has been a marked difference in aid between bilateral and multilateral donors in this context. In this period, multilateral donors allocated more than 62 percent of their total aid to low-income countries, while bilateral donors gave only about 41 percent of their total aid to this group. In addition, lower-middle-income countries received about 30 percent of the total bilateral aid and 22 percent of the multilateral aid between 2001 and 2007. The share of foreign aid going to upper-middle-income and high-income countries has been declining since the 1970s, but the share of unallocated aid has been increasing.

TABLE 3.2 Allocation of official development assistance by income group, 1971–2007 (percentage of total allocated funds)

Income group	1971–80	1981–90	1991–2000	2001–07
		All donors		
Low-income	42.2	44.6	42.8	45.9
Lower-middle-income	30.2	27.1	30.3	28.0
Upper-middle-income	5.3	5.2	4.3	3.4
MADCTs	6.7	5.8	3.4	0.1
Unallocated by income	15.7	17.4	19.2	22.7
Total	100.0	100.0	100.0	100.0
		Bilateral DAC donors		
Low-income	45.7	40.6	36.3	41.2
Lower-middle-income	25.5	27.8	31.1	30.4
Upper-middle-income	5.2	6.0	4.5	2.9
MADCTs	10.4	8.3	4.6	0.0
Unallocated by income	13.1	17.3	23.5	25.5
Total	100.0	100.0	100.0	100.0
		Multilateral donors		
Low-income	57.4	66.5	59.8	62.3
Lower-middle-income	25.1	18.8	27.0	21.7
Upper-middle-income	6.8	2.8	2.8	4.4
MADCTs	1.8	0.6	0.5	0.2
Unallocated by income	8.7	11.2	9.8	11.4
Total	100.0	100.0	100.0	100.0

SOURCE: OECD, Development Database on Aid from DAC Members: DAC Online (various years).

NOTES: DAC: Development Assistance Committee; MADCT: more advanced developing countries and territories.

Sectoral Allocation of Aid

Figure 3.5 shows the dynamics of sectoral allocation of ODA commitments between 1973 and 2002. It is clear from this figure that on average about two-thirds of total aid in this period was sector allocable. The most important observation from Figure 3.5 is that the share of development aid going to social infrastructure and services has doubled since the mid-1970s, reaching about two-thirds of the total sector-allocable ODA, or more than 40 percent of total ODA commitments. At the same time, the share of ODA allocated to the economic infrastructure and production sectors dropped significantly. In particular, aid to the production sectors (including agriculture, industry, trade, and tourism) decreased about threefold, dropping from a high of about 28–29 percent in the early 1980s to about 7–9 percent in recent years.

The main reason behind the fall in aid flows to production sectors in developing countries was a declining commitment to agriculture from bilateral donors, especially multilateral agencies including the World Bank. As a result, the share of agriculture in ODA declined about five to six times over the past two decades (Figure 3.6). It also declined in absolute terms, from a high of $8.3 billion to $3.4 billion (in 2004 dollars). A combination of political and economic factors explains the decline of donor commitment to agriculture. The economic reasons include failed agricultural development efforts and unsuccessful interventions in the sector that led to poor performance of the World Bank and other donor-supported projects. The falling international commodity

FIGURE 3.5 Sectoral allocation of official development assistance (ODA) commitments, 1973–2002

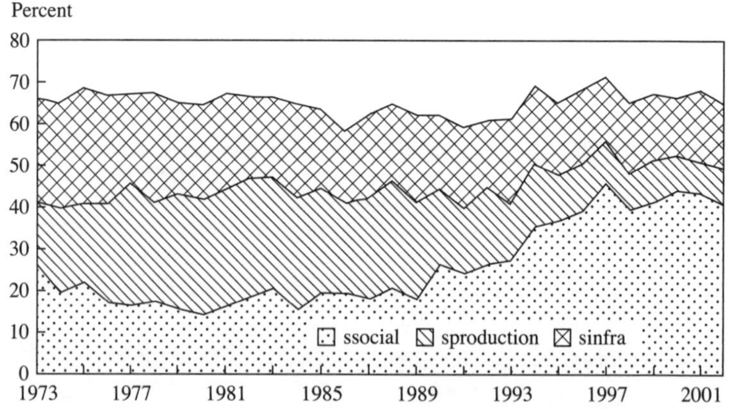

SOURCE: OECD, Development Database on Aid Activities: CRS Online (various years).
NOTES: ssocial: share of ODA to the social sector; sproduction: share of ODA to the production sector; sinfra: share of ODA to economic infrastructure.

FIGURE 3.6 Official development assistance (ODA) to agriculture, 1973–2007

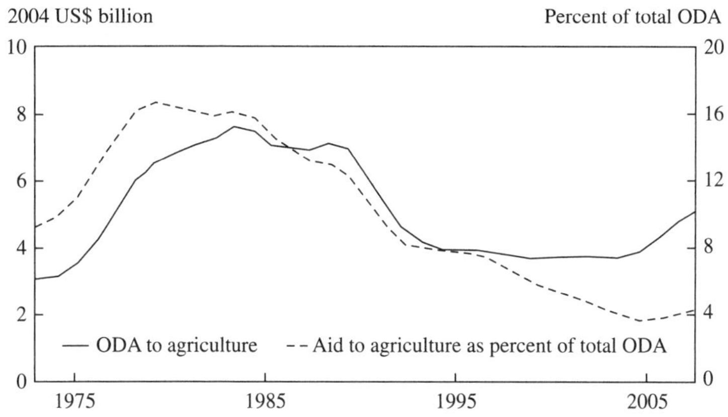

SOURCE: OECD, Development Database on Aid Activities: CRS Online (various years).
NOTE: ODA to agriculture is smoothed using a locally weighted regression.

prices contributed to this failure by making agriculture less profitable. The political factors include pressure groups in both donor and recipient countries, including domestic farm groups in donor countries that were opposed to supporting agriculture in their main export markets and environmentalist groups that saw agriculture as a contributor to environmental problems. Increased commitment to the social sector and the need for emergency responses to numerous crises also contributed to declining support for the production sectors, including agriculture (World Bank 2007).

In response to recent political and economic events and advances in development thinking, donor interest in agriculture has increased. As a result, ODA to agriculture has slightly increased in recent years. The share of agriculture in ODA increased to 5.2 percent in 2007 from 3.5 percent in 2004. It also increased in absolute terms, from less than $3.4 billion in 2004 to $5.2 billion (in 2004 dollars) in 2007 (Figure 3.6).

Variable Definitions and Descriptive Statistics

Descriptive statistics of all variables used in the study are provided in Appendix D. This section briefly describes the dependent variables (DVs) and key IVs. As noted earlier, analysis of aid effectiveness includes three equations: growth, investment, and human capital. Although the DV in the human capital equation measures secondary school enrollment, the DV in the growth equation is the growth rate ($g_{j,t}$) of real GNI per capita ($Y_{j,t}$). Further, the DV in the investment equation is the investment ratio ($INV_{j,t}$), which is measured as the ratio of total investment ($I_{j,t}$) to GNI in a given time period. Specifically, for an aid recipient country *j* in time period *t,* these variables are, respectively, computed as follows:

$$g_{j,t} = \frac{Y_{j,t} - Y_{j,t-1}}{Y_{j,t-1}} \tag{3.1}$$

and

$$INV_{j,t} = \frac{I_{j,t}}{GNI_{j,t}}. \tag{3.2}$$

The DVs relevant to the aid allocation model are computed as follows. The first divides the total ODA commitments of each donor to a given recipient in real terms ($TODA_{i,j,t}$) by the recipient's population ($POP_{j,t}$) to express them on a per capita ($AIDP_{i,j,t}$) basis:

$$AIDP_{i,j,t} = \frac{TODA_{i,j,t}}{POP_{j,t}}. \tag{3.3}$$

Per capita aid commitments to the production sectors ($PAIDP_{i,j,t}$), the social sector ($SAIDP_{i,j,t}$), and economic infrastructure ($IAIDP_{i,j,t}$) in real terms are constructed in a similar way:

$$PAIDP_{i,j,t} = \frac{PODA_{i,j,t}}{POP_{i,j,t}}, \tag{3.4}$$

$$SAIDP_{i,j,t} = \frac{SODA_{i,j,t}}{POP_{j,t}}, \text{ and} \tag{3.5}$$

$$IAIDP_{i,j,t} = \frac{IODA_{i,j,t}}{POP_{j,t}}. \tag{3.6}$$

The key IVs related to the estimation of aid effectiveness are the relative measures of total aid ($AID_{j,t}$) for economic uses ($EAID_{j,t}$), including aid to economic infrastructure ($IAID_{j,t}$) and social aid ($SAID_{j,t}$), with respect to a recipient's GDP. Specifically, for country *j* and time period *t,* the ratios of aid to the production, social, and economic infrastructure sectors are computed, respectively, as follows:

$$AID_{j,t} = \frac{TOAD_{j,t}}{GPD_{j,t}}, \tag{3.7}$$

$$EAID_{j,t} = \frac{EOAD_{j,t}}{GPD_{j,t}}, \tag{3.8}$$

$$SAID_{j,t} = \frac{SODA_{j,t}}{GDP_{j,t}}, \text{ and} \tag{3.9}$$

$$IAID_{j,t} = \frac{IODA_{j,t}}{GDP_{j,t}}, \tag{3.10}$$

where $EOAD_{j,t}$, $SOAD_{j,t}$, and $IOAD_{j,t}$ are total ODA allocated for economic uses, social aid, and aid to economic infrastructure, respectively. As mentioned earlier, the interactions of these variables with governance enter respective equations as key IVs.

The descriptive analysis of the data shows that the raw data have a lot of noise and fluctuations. This is not a problem for cross-section regressions because they use annual averages, with the averages taken over the period 1973–2002. Concerning dynamic panel regressions, the literature suggests that to reduce the short-term fluctuations and the noise in the data, one can use four- or five-year averages (Baldacci et al. 2004; Durlauf, Johnson, and Temple 2005). Therefore, in dynamic panel regressions I use five-year averages of the variables in estimating the equations. For example, the first observation is the average over the period 1973–77, followed by the average over the period 1978–82, and so forth. It should also be clear that although conceptually distinct, skewed distributions and outliers have similar consequences for an estimator in terms of the robustness of both validity and efficiency. Under these distributional circumstances, robust regression that is resistant to the influence of outliers may be the reasonable recourse. It does not make any assumptions about the distribution and takes distributional circumstances into account using so-called sandwich estimators for the standard errors.

Another key IV is the quality of governance. As discussed elsewhere in this book, there are many aspects of governance that may matter for aid effectiveness, and thus for aid allocation. Ideally we would like to account for all possible dimensions in order to avoid estimation problems. However, this is not a feasible approach because of the lack of sufficient degrees of freedom and reliable data. Therefore, we need governance measures that have long time runs and wide country coverage and that are highly correlated with other dimensions of governance. Two widely used governance indicators provided by Freedom House—political rights and civil liberties—met the previously mentioned criteria, and data on them are available for many countries over a long time period (1972 to today). These indicators correlate between 0.55 and 0.94 with the six composite indicators of Kaufmann, Kraay, and Zoido-Lobaton (2003). The canonical correlation between these six indicators and the two Freedom House measures is 0.96. Klitgaard, Fedderke, and Akramov (2005) also suggest that these two indicators consistently "correlated highly" with many other governance indicators. Therefore, the simple combination of these two indicators is used to control for democratic quality of governance.

The general characteristics of the values of these categorical variables and some exemplary countries are presented in Appendix E. For use in empirical analyses, political rights and civil liberties indicators are combined and then reversed symmetrically, resulting in a new democracy variable with scales from 1 to 7. Therefore, the higher scores are associated with better-quality democratic governance. The descriptive analysis shows that the average democratic quality of governance (standardized normal mean for all recipients) improved from 1975 to 2000. The analysis of the relationship between total aid per capita and the quality of governance in recipient countries indicates that there was strong heterogeneity across recipient countries. There was a positive correlation for 48 recipient countries, a negative correlation for 22 recipients, and no statistically significant correlation for 72 countries.

One may argue that these indicators are not objective measures; therefore, they describe only perceptions about the democratic quality of governance. However, even though Freedom House's indicators are subjective measures, they may still provide reasonable signals about the quality of governance across countries and were constructed applying the same procedures for all countries. Therefore, they can be accepted as plausible proxy measures of the democratic quality of governance. Another concern is that even if these indicators somehow measure or proxy the actual democratic quality of governance in recipient countries, they describe only one dimension of governance, that is, the dimension of democracy. However, as mentioned earlier, these two governance indicators correlate reasonably well with other governance indicators, including the composite governance measures provided by Kaufmann, Kraay, and Zoido-Lobaton (2003). These strong correlations suggest that these indicators of governance measure very similar things. Therefore, it can be assumed that a latent governance variable that is constructed from political rights and civil liberties indicators is a reasonable proxy for the overall quality of governance.[4]

Further, to account for potential nonlinearities in the relationship between aid and democratic governance, I distinguish between different categories of democratic governance using Freedom House's typology, which classifies countries into three categories: free countries, or full democracies; partially free countries; and countries that are not free, or autocratic. This typology, which approximates three levels of democratic governance, allows us to investigate the nonlinear relationship between governance and aid flows. Figure 3.7 demonstrates the dynamics of the average democracy score for each of these three groups of countries. Three decades ago, most developing countries were very similar in terms of democratic governance. However, over time some of these countries experienced transitions from authoritarian regimes to more open

4. Nevertheless, these two indexes do not cover the meaning of *governance,* although they are the best we have and they are closely correlated with other governance variables. Therefore, the results should be viewed with some caution.

FIGURE 3.7 Average democracy scores in free, partially free, and not free (autocratic) countries

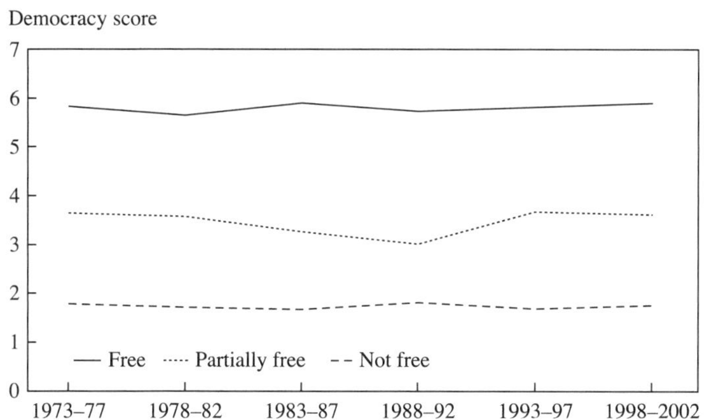

SOURCE: Freedom House (2009).
NOTES: Average democracy scores are calculated using political rights and civil liberties indicators from Freedom House's Freedom in the World database (Freedom House 2009). These indicators measure the wider state of freedom in a country, reflecting both governmental and nongovernmental constraints. Although they do not explicitly measure democratic performance, they measure rights and freedoms integral to democracy. The political rights and civil liberties scores are combined and averaged, then reversed symmetrically, resulting in a new democracy variable with a scale from 1 to 7. Therefore, higher scores are associated with a better quality of democratic governance.

and democratic governance systems by establishing transparent and accountable governments.

This chapter provides sources and definitions of key variables used in this study. It also discusses the basic descriptive statistics for the data I use in the analysis of donors' aid allocation decisions and the relationship between different components of foreign aid and economic growth. The results of these analyses are provided in the following two chapters.

4 Aid Allocation

Aggregate patterns, such as those shown in Przeworski et al. (2000), suggest that the relationship between the level of economic development and the democratic quality of governance is strong and robust. Therefore, with few exceptions, one can plausibly predict the quality of governance in a given country just by looking at the level of its per capita income or vice versa. In this context, the typology of countries based on the quality of governance developed in the previous chapter can be considered as a proxy for the level of economic development. The important question, however, has to do with the relative importance of the quality of governance to aid effectiveness and allocation. The main hypothesis of this study is that development aid will have a different impact on economic growth depending on its sectoral allocation and the type (level) of governance in a given recipient country. This chapter discusses the theoretical and empirical issues related to aid allocation, with special attention to the quality of democratic governance, and then presents the results of an empirical analysis. A discussion of the effectiveness of aid in this context is provided in the next chapter.

Analytical Framework and Empirical Methodology

The theoretical discussion provided in Appendix F suggests that donors need to find a way to improve their information system regarding recipient governments. This will allow them to better maximize the utility they can expect from the allocation of foreign aid; that is, improvements in donors' information structure increase allocative efficiency. In this regard, the quality of governance in aid recipient countries has recently moved into the spotlight of official donor agencies, both bilateral and multilateral. The rationale is that rewarding some recipients for good governance will create better incentives for their peers. Therefore, governance should be explicitly included as a key independent variable in empirical analysis.

Consider the deterministic aid allocation model widely used in the literature (for example, see Trumbull and Wall 1994), which assumes that in each time period t, each donor country i allocates its foreign aid budget $Y_{i,t}$ among N

recipient countries with the objective of maximizing the weighted sum of the total impacts of the donor's assistance to the recipient countries. The most important assumption of the model is that all donors have the same subjective measure of the impact of aid to a recipient, that is, all donors use the same set of weights (w_j) with respect to individual donors. However, these weights vary for individual donors based on the relative importance of a given recipient to the donor. The degree of relative importance is determined by historic, strategic, and geographic factors. Suppressing the time dimension, the per capita impact of aid (h_j) in recipient j is a function of the per capita aid received (a_j), per capita well-being or income (x_j), and population size (N_j):

$$h_j = \frac{a_j^{\beta}}{x_j^{\gamma} N_j^{\tau}}\ ; 0 < \beta < 1,\ 0 < |\gamma| < 1,\ 0 \leq \tau < 1. \tag{4.1}$$

Donors expect (or hope) that the total impact of aid will increase as per capita aid increases. The effect of recipients' well-being (income) on the total impact of aid might be positive if aid is considered as a complement to low levels of well-being (income) or negative if aid is considered as a substitute for low levels of well-being (income). Donors might expect that it will be easier to make a positive impact on smaller countries, so the expected effect of the size of a recipient's population on the impact of per capita aid is negative.

Therefore, each donor faces the following problem:

$$\max_{a_{ij}} H_i = \frac{w_j a_{ij}^{\beta}}{x_i^{Y} N_j^{\tau}} \tag{4.2}$$

subject to budget constraint

$$\Sigma_j a_{ij} = Y_i. \tag{4.3}$$

Assuming that the aid received from various donors is perfectly fungible, and applying the method of Lagrange, the previous maximization problem can be solved to obtain the equilibrium values of the marginal effect of an increase in the aid budget and of per capita aid for each year to each donor (Trumbull and Wall 1994). Introducing the time dimension and making the log transformation and some algebraic transformations, one can obtain the following linear form:

$$\log a_{jt}^{*} = \alpha_0 + \alpha_1 \log X_{jt} + \alpha_2 N_{jt} + \eta_j + \mu_t, \tag{4.4}$$

where a sign (*) indicates equilibrium values. Because the aid allocation decisions are independent for each time period, the period effect (μ_t) is the same for all recipient countries within a given year. However, recipient countries are assigned different weights; therefore, there are recipient effects (η_j) that are fixed over time. Consequently, Equation 4.4 allows one to account for unobserved recipient and period effects.

The aid allocation literature estimates some modifications of Equation 4.4 while explicitly controlling for donors' self-interest and recipients' needs to explain aid allocation policies. As noted earlier, the most important assumption in Equation 4.4 is that all donors have the same subjective measure of the impact of aid on a recipient. This is a very strict assumption. However, there may be differences between donors in measuring the impact of aid with respect to different recipients. There are many factors that might lead to these differences in donor policies. For example, these differences might be a product of the countries' past colonial relationship, or some donors might give greater importance to certain regions or countries based on geographic or strategic considerations. In this regard, Alesina and Dollar (2000) provide different parameter estimates for individual bilateral donors. Berthélemy and Tichit (2004), using a random-effects tobit model, and Berthélemy (2006a), using a three-dimensional panel approach within a two-part model framework, have provided the proper tests of differences among bilateral donors.

The important methodological issue in examining aid allocation patterns is to select an appropriate estimation technique that allows for the correction of potential biases that occur from sample selection. The sample includes both recipients and nonrecipients of aid from the bilateral donors under consideration. Therefore, some of the bilateral aid flows are equal to zero, because donors tend to allocate aid only to specific targeted countries. Consequently, we deal with a censored variable, which implies that estimates are flawed if we model average aid, including the zeros. A misleading regression model will be fitted, because zero outcomes are the result of a nonrandom aid allocation process. Consider an alternative approach, which assumes excluding non–aid recipients from the sample. This truncates the error term if the donors have systematically used some criteria to partition aid recipients from nonrecipients and thus violates the important assumption that the error term is zero. The aid allocation literature uses three different limited variable-modeling techniques that allow us to model the data with censored character: a two-part model, Heckman's two-step method, and a Type 1 Tobit model. Each of these estimation techniques has its own strengths and weaknesses.

This study uses a two-part model: in the first step, a probability model determines the likelihood of giving aid (selection equation), and in the second step, a cross-sectional panel (difference-in-difference) model, conditional only on strictly positive aid commitments, explains aggregate aid flows (aggregate aid allocation equation). This procedure assumes that the choice of a recipient is independent of the amount allocated to that recipient in the second step. The selection equation is estimated using probit and random-effects probit techniques, while the allocation equation is estimated using standard least squares or time-series cross-sectional generalized least squares estimation techniques.

Further, aggregate aid commitments are disaggregated into sectoral aid commitments, and then the determinants of per capita sectoral aid flows are examined (sectoral aid allocation equation). Again, one cannot safely use ordinary estimation techniques to estimate the sectoral aid allocation model because some donors tend to allocate aid only to specific targeted sectors; that is, we again deal with a censored variable. Therefore, I estimate the sectoral aid allocation model by using standard Tobit and cross-sectional time-series Tobit techniques. This model assumes that the independent variables have an equal impact on the probability of receiving aid for a given sector and the amount of aid allocated thereafter.

As discussed earlier, bilateral aid allocation decisions are explained by both donors' self-interest and recipients' needs. Therefore, recipients' per capita income and life expectancy are included in the model as measures of recipients' needs, while political similarities and trade links (exports from donors to recipients) between donors and recipients are included as measures of donors' interests. Recipients' population size and the so-called bandwagon effect are included in the model to control for potential scale economies. The bandwagon effect is seen when a donor provides aid to a particular recipient because many other donors do the same. In other words, the bandwagon effect arises when a donor's preference for a recipient increases as the amount of aid given by other donors increases. In the sectoral allocation equation, some macroeconomic variables are also included to see whether sectoral aid flows are affected by macroeconomic conditions of recipients. The model does not explicitly control for time-invariant characteristics in donor–recipient relationships, such as their colonial background and ethnic and religious fractionalizations, but the identification strategy described later allows us to implicitly control for fixed relationships between donors and recipients.

As mentioned earlier, an important objective is to evaluate the effect of governance on donors' aid allocation decisions. Therefore, using the insights of the theoretical discussion in Appendix F, the quality of governance is introduced into all three equations. If donors believe that aid is put to good use in countries with better governance, the total impact of aid increases with better quality of governance. Therefore, it can be expected that donors will allocate more aid to countries with better governance, other things equal; that is, the marginal impact of governance on per capita aid should be positive.

Identifying this effect, in addition to controlling for donors' interests, recipients' needs, and other variables, requires controlling for any systematic shocks to foreign aid flows that are correlated with, but not due to, the quality of recipients' governance. This is done in three ways in the two-part estimation described earlier. First, period effects are included to capture any global trends in foreign aid flows. Second, donor fixed effects are included to account for time-invariant differences in donor aid allocation policies. Third, recipient fixed effects are included to control for time-invariant recipient effects and differences in donors' behavior toward individual recipient countries. That is, the model identifies the pure effect of the governance variable on bilateral foreign aid flows.

Based on these considerations, Equation 4.4 is revised by introducing a donor subscript, governance, donor effects, and other control variables. The following specification of the aid allocation equation allows us to estimate the marginal effects of the three groups of independent variables on aid allocation while isolating unobserved donor, recipient, and period effects:

$$Aid_{i,j,t} = \alpha_{0+\alpha 1} Z_{i,j,t} + \alpha_2 X_{j,t} + \alpha_3 (GOV)_{j,t} + \delta_i + \eta_j + \mu_t + \gamma_{i,j,t}, \qquad (4.5)$$

where

- Z is a matrix of time-variant strategic and economic relationships between a donor and a recipient. This includes donors' exports to recipient countries and political similarities between donors and recipients as revealed by their voting behavior in the UN General Assembly.
- X is a matrix of time-variant control variables for recipient country j at time t. These include per capita GDP, population size, life expectancy at birth, amount of aid received from other donors, military grants received from the United States, a dummy variable for a failed state, and so on.
- *GOV* denotes the key independent variable, which is quality of governance. For these purposes, institutional and democratic measures of the quality of governance are used.
- δ_i, η_j, and μ_t are donor-, recipient-, and time-specific effects.

In this model, donors' aid allocation decisions are motivated by two broad groups of rationales for providing foreign aid: donors' self-interest (strategic, political, and economic) and altruism or recipients' needs (donors' desire to promote welfare and economic development in developing countries). Further, the quality of governance enters the model as an information signal that allows donors to make judgments about the potential efficiency with which their aid will be used.

Equation 4.5 specifies the aggregate aid allocation model. The aid eligibility and sectoral aid allocation equations are also specified in a similar way. As discussed elsewhere, the dependent variables are different at each stage. In the eligibility equation, the dependent variable is a binary decision variable based on whether or not a country is deemed eligible to receive aid. Following the common usage in the aid allocation literature, it is assumed that a country is eligible to receive aid if it is given any positive amount of aid. At the aggregate aid allocation stage, donors decide how much aid to allocate to a given recipient country. Therefore, the dependent variable in the aggregate aid allocation equation is the actual level of aid allocated to a given aid-eligible country. At the sectoral aid allocation stage, donors allocate aid among different sectors. In this research, three subparts of aggregate aid are distinguished: aid to the production sectors, aid to the social sector, and aid to economic infrastructure. Therefore, three sectoral aid allocation equations are estimated with the following dependent variables: per capita aid to the production sectors, per capita aid to social sector, and per capita aid to economic infrastructure.

Empirical Results

The regression results are reported in Tables 4.1–4.5. I use five-year averages of the variables during the 1973–2002 horizon in estimating these regression equations. I deal with three-dimensional (time period, donor, and recipient) panel data from potentially about 10,000 observations. However, the number of observations varies depending on the availability of explanatory variables. I start with results from a simpler standard model, such as a probit (eligibility equation) and OLS (aid allocation equation) model. Then I compare these results with results from more sophisticated estimations. The robustness of the results is checked by estimating alternative models using more sophisticated estimation techniques such as random-effects probit (eligibility equation) and feasible generalized least squares (aggregate aid allocation equation) and random-effects tobit (sector allocation equations) and controlling for donor, recipient, and time fixed effects.

Aid Eligibility Stage

The estimated coefficients suggest that recipients' democratic quality of governance positively influences the likelihood of their being eligible for foreign aid. By using probit results, one may suggest that countries with poor democratic governance (not free countries or autocracies) have about a 0.2 percentage point (associated with an estimated coefficient of –1.05, Table 4.1, probit model 2) lower probability of receiving foreign aid than do countries with high levels of democratic governance (free countries or democracies), all other things equal. Similarly, countries with medium levels of democratic governance (partially free countries) have about a 0.16 percentage point (associated with an estimated coefficient of –0.79) lower probability of receiving foreign aid. These effects would not change much if one were to consider the results of the random-effects probit estimators with recipients as an independent unit and donor and period fixed effects (Table 4.1, random-effects probit models 1–4). Therefore, we can conclude that the democratic quality of governance positively influences the eligibility of developing countries for foreign aid. With respect to the institutional quality of governance, the probit model shows that it also positively affects the dependent variable, but its marginal impact on the probability of aid eligibility is very small. Moreover, the random-effects probit model indicates that the marginal effect of the institutional quality of governance on aid eligibility is virtually none. Therefore, one cannot reject the null hypothesis that institutional quality of governance has no effect on aid eligibility.

As different specifications of random-effects probit models suggest, on average, population size plays a positive role in aid eligibility decisions at the

TABLE 4.1 Aid eligibility equation, all bilateral donors (dependent variable: eligibility dummy)

	Probit			Random-effects probit			
	1	2	3	1	2	3	4
GDP per capita (log)	–0.60***	–0.62***	–0.55***	–0.44***	–0.46***	–0.42***	–0.43***
	(0.04)	(0.04)	(0.03)	(0.08)	(0.08)	(0.08)	(0.06)
Population (log)	–0.10***	–0.05	–0.002	0.26***	0.30***	0.30***	0.25***
	(0.03)	(0.03)	(0.02)	(0.07)	(0.06)	(0.06)	(0.05)
Life expectancy (log)	–0.27	–0.1	–0.13	–0.33	–0.28	–0.43	–0.46
	(0.21)	(0.2)	(0.16)	(0.43)	(0.42)	(0.30)	(0.36)
Exports (log)	0.34***	0.34***	0.33***	0.23***	0.23***	0.25***	0.22***
	(0.02)	(0.02)	(0.01)	(0.03)	(0.03)	(0.02)	(0.02)
Bandwagon effect (log)	0.06*	0.15***	0.11***	0.37***	0.45***	0.32***	0.30***
	(0.03)	(0.03)	(0.02)	(0.07)	(0.06)	(0.04)	(0.03)
US military grants (log)	–0.04***	–0.04***	–0.04***	0.001	–0.001	–0.01	
	(0.01)	(0.01)	(0.01)	(0.02)	(0.02)	(0.02)	
Political similarity	–0.18*	–0.13*		0.04	–0.06		
	(0.10)	(0.10)		(0.31)	(0.30)		
Failed-state dummy	0.06	0.11*	0.13***	–0.06	0.003	0.02	0.07
	(0.07)	(0.07)	(0.05)	(0.11)	(0.11)	(0.08)	(0.07)

Institutional quality	0.02***	0.03***	0.02***	–0.02*	–0.02	–0.01	–0.01
	(0.005)	(0.005)	(0.004)	(0.01)	(0.01)	(0.01)	(0.01)
Democratic quality	0.13***			0.1***			
	(0.01)			(0.02)			
Not free (low)		–1.05***	–0.90***		–1.11***	–1.07***	–1.02***
		(0.09)	(0.06)		(0.2)	(0.13)	(0.14)
Partially free (medium)		–0.79***	–0.52***		–0.91***	–0.62***	–0.62***
		(0.1)	(0.06)		(0.2)	(0.12)	(0.16)
Constant	6.95	5.17	4.53	7.97	6.52	6.52	2.71
Donor fixed effects				Yes	Yes	Yes	Yes
Period fixed effects				Yes	Yes	Yes	Yes
Number of recipients	98	99	99	98	99	101	105
Number of observations	4,526	4,562	7,806	4,526	4,562	7,806	9,558

SOURCES: Author's estimations using data from IMF (2006), Freedom House (2009), Gartzke (2010), World Bank (2010), and OECD, Development Database on Aid from DAC Members: DAC Online (various years).

NOTES: Standard errors are in parentheses. An empty cell indicates that the corresponding variable is not included in the model. Log means a variable is in logarithmic form. All model specifications control for recipient fixed effects. Observations are five-year averages during the 1973–2002 horizon. * indicates significant at the 10 percent level; ** indicates significant at the 5 percent level; *** indicates significant at the 1 percent level.

TABLE 4.2 Aggregate aid allocation equation, all bilateral donors (dependent variable: log of per capita aggregate aid commitments)

	OLS	DDD1	DDD2	DDD3	DDD4	FGLS1	FGLS2
GDP per capita (log)	–0.96***	–1.06***	–1.09***	–1.07***	–1.10***	–0.79***	–0.77***
	(0.05)	(0.07)	(0.07)	(0.06)	(0.05)	(0.05)	(0.03)
Population (log)	–0.77***	–0.85***	–0.86***	–0.81***	–0.86***	–0.60***	–0.59***
	(0.04)	(0.06)	(0.06)	(0.04)	(0.04)	(0.04)	(0.03)
Life expectancy	–0.03***	–0.02***	–0.02***	–0.02***	–0.01***	–0.03***	–0.03***
	(0.01)	(0.01)	(0.01)	(0.005)	(0.005)	(0.004)	(0.003)
Exports (log)	0.82***	0.71***	0.72***	0.68***	0.70***	0.61***	0.54***
	(0.02)	(0.03)	(0.03)	(0.02)	(0.02)	(0.02)	(0.02)
Bandwagon effect (log)	0.67***	0.39***	0.40***	0.36***	0.41***	0.76***	0.61***
	(0.05)	(0.06)	(0.06)	(0.04)	(0.04)	(0.04)	(0.02)
US military grants (log)	–0.05***	0.02	0.04**		0.02*	0.01	
	(0.02)	(0.02)	(0.02)		(0.01)	(0.01)	
Political similarity	–1.25***	–0.76***	–0.79***			–0.85***	
	(0.10)	(0.19)	(0.19)			(0.18)	
Failed-state dummy	0.06		–0.14	–0.02		0.05	0.15***
	(0.08)		(0.08)	0.06		(0.07)	(0.05)
Institutional quality	0.02**	0.01	0.01	0.01**		0.01	0.02***
	(0.01)	(0.01)	(0.01)	(0.006)		(0.01)	(0.005)

Democratic quality	0.11***	0.08***					
	(0.01)	(0.01)					
Not free (low)			–0.81***	–0.95***	–0.73***	–0.88***	–0.90***
			(0.18)	(0.14)	(0.12)	(0.09)	(0.06)
Partially free (medium)			–0.25	–0.23*	–0.14	–0.43***	–0.27***
			(0.17)	(0.13)	(0.11)	(0.09)	(0.06)
Constant	9.67	15.19				10.04	3.87
	(0.67)	(1.20)				(1.02)	(0.46)
R-squared	0.48	0.71	0.73	0.59	0.59		
Donor fixed effects		Yes	Yes	Yes	Yes	Yes	Yes
Period fixed effects		Yes	Yes	Yes	Yes	Yes	Yes
Number of recipients	98	98	99	105	133	99	105
Number of observations	3,778	3,778	3,801	7,664	8,485	3,801	7,664

SOURCES: Author's estimations using data from IMF (2006), Freedom House (2009), Gartzke (2010), World Bank (2010), and OECD, Development Database on Aid from DAC Members: DAC Online (various years).

NOTES: Standard errors are in parentheses. An empty cell indicates that the corresponding variable is not included in the model. Log means a variable is in logarithmic form. OLS: ordinary least squares; DDD: difference-in-difference-in-differences; FGLS: feasible generalized least squares. All models control for recipient fixed effects. Observations are five-year averages during the 1973–2002 horizon. * indicates significant at the 10 percent level; ** indicates significant at the 5 percent level; *** indicates significant at the 1 percent level.

TABLE 4.3 Sectoral aid allocation equation: Social infrastructure and services, all bilateral donors (dependent variable: log of per capita aid to social sectors)

	Tobit	RET1	RET2	RET3
GDP per capita (log)	–0.61***	–0.63***	–0.72***	–0.67***
	(0.06)	(0.07)	(0.08)	(0.08)
Population (log)	–0.55***	–0.54***	–0.64***	–0.58
	(0.04)	(0.04)	(0.05)	(0.05)
Life expectancy (log)	0.003	0.002	0.003	0.003
	(0.005)	(0.007)	(0.007)	(0.01)
Exports (log)	0.41***	0.44***	0.51***	0.49***
	(0.02)	(0.02)	(0.03)	(0.03)
Bandwagon effect (log)	0.01***	0.002	0.001	0.001
	(0.003)	(0.01)	(0.003)	(0.003)
Inflation	0.000**	0.000**	0.000***	0.000***
	(0.000)	(0.000)	(0.000)	(0.000)
Financial depth			0.001	
			(0.002)	
Failed-state dummy	–0.07	–0.11	–0.11	–0.13
	(0.08)	(0.08)	(0.08)	(0.08)
Institutional quality	0.04***	0.01	0.02	0.01
	(0.01)	(0.01)	(0.01)	(0.01)
Democratic quality				
Not free (low)	–0.53***	–0.49***	–0.53***	–0.47***
	(0.12)	(0.17)	(0.16)	(0.17)
Partially free (medium)	–0.02	–0.09	–0.10	–0.08
	(0.11)	(0.15)	(0.15)	(0.16)
Constant	7.16	7.4	9.58	7.75
	(0.52)	(0.68)	(0.82)	(0.81)
Period fixed effects		Yes	Yes	Yes
Number of recipients	105	105	102	105
Number of observations	5,678	5,678	5,429	5,678

SOURCES: Author's estimations using data from IMF (2006), Freedom House (2009), Gartzke (2010), World Bank (2010), and OECD, Development Database on Aid Activities: CRS Online (various years).

NOTES: Standard errors are in parentheses. An empty cell indicates that the corresponding variable is not included in the model. Log means a variable is in logarithmic form. RET: random-effects tobit. All RET model specifications include donor and recipient fixed effects. Observations are five-year averages during the 1973–2002 horizon. * indicates significant at the 10 percent level; ** indicates significant at the 5 percent level; *** indicates significant at the 1 percent level.

aggregate level. As expected, per capita income has a significant and negative effect on aid eligibility, which suggests that donors are more likely to select poorer countries, but life expectancy seems to be insignificant in donors' decision-making if one controls for per capita income. On average, donors seem more likely to give aid to their trade partners than to countries that are not trade partners. The estimates also suggest that the so-called bandwagon effects have a

TABLE 4.4 Sectoral aid allocation equation: Production sector, all bilateral donors (dependent variable: log of per capita aid to production sectors)

	Tobit	RET1	RET2	RET3
GDP per capita (log)	–0.39***	–0.41***	–0.52***	–0.46***
	(0.04)	(0.05)	(0.06)	(0.05)
Population (log)	–0.31***	–0.28***	–0.35***	–0.32***
	(0.02)	(0.03)	(0.03)	(0.03)
Life expectancy (log)	–0.02***	–0.003	–0.002	–0.004
	(0.004)	(0.005)	(0.005)	(0.006)
Exports (log)	0.37***	0.33***	0.39***	0.38***
	(0.02)	(0.01)	(0.02)	(0.02)
Bandwagon effect (log)	0.01***	0.01***	0.01***	0.01***
	(0.001)	(0.001)	(0.001)	(0.001)
Inflation	0.000	0.000	0.000	0.000
	(0.000)	(0.000)	(0.000)	(0.000)
Financial depth	–0.004***	–0.003***	–0.001	–0.003***
	(0.001)	(0.001)	(0.001)	(0.001)
Trade openness			–0.002*	
			(0.001)	
Failed-state dummy	–0.11*	–0.10	–0.12**	–0.10*
	(0.06)	(0.06)	(0.06)	(0.06)
Institutional quality	0.01	–0.002	–0.001	–0.003
	(0.01)	(0.01)	(0.01)	(0.01)
Democratic quality				
Not free (low)	–0.33***	–0.19*	–0.24**	–0.21*
	(0.08)	(0.11)	(0.11)	(0.11)
Partially free (medium)	0.02	0.01	0.02	–0.01
	(0.08)	(0.01)	(0.1)	(0.01)
Constant	5.01	4.43	5.47	4.75
	(0.35)	(0.46)	(0.57)	(0.59)
Period fixed effects	None	Yes	Yes	Yes
Number of recipients	104	104	102	104
Number of observations	5,529	5,529	5,429	5,529

SOURCES: Author's estimations using data from IMF (2006), Freedom House (2009), Gartzke (2010), World Bank (2010), and OECD, Development Database on Aid Activities: CRS Online (various years).

NOTES: Standard errors are in parentheses. An empty cell indicates that the corresponding variable is not included in the model. Log means a variable is in logarithmic form. RET: random-effects tobit. All RET model specifications include donor and recipient fixed effects. Observations are five-year averages during the 1973–2002 horizon. * indicates significant at the 10 percent level; ** indicates significant at the 5 percent level; *** indicates significant at the 1 percent level.

TABLE 4.5 Sectoral aid allocation equation: Economic infrastructure, all bilateral donors (dependent variable: log of per capita aid to economic infrastructure)

	Tobit	RET1	RET2	RET3
GDP per capita (log)	–0.56***	–0.64***	–0.71***	–0.66***
	(0.05)	(0.09)	(0.1)	(0.09)
Population (log)	–0.34***	–0.41***	–0.48***	–0.43***
	(0.03)	(0.05)	(0.09)	(0.05)
Life expectancy (log)	–0.01	0.002	0.002	–0.000
	(0.01)	(0.01)	(0.01)	(0.000)
Exports (log)	0.47***	0.53***	0.60***	0.57***
	(0.02)	(0.02)	(0.03)	(0.03)
Bandwagon effect (log)	0.01***	0.01***	0.01***	0.01***
	(0.002)	(0.002)	(0.003)	(0.003)
Inflation	0.000	0.000	0.000	0.000
	(0.000)	(0.000)	(0.000)	(0.000)
Financial depth	–0.004***	–0.004***	–0.001	–0.004***
	(0.001)	(0.001)	(0.001)	(0.001)
Trade openness			–0.003	
			(0.002)	
Failed-state dummy	–0.08	–0.16*	–0.17	–0.14
	(0.08)	(0.1)	(0.12)	(0.1)
Institutional quality	0.01	–0.01	–0.01	–0.01
	(0.01)	(0.01)	(0.01)	(0.01)
Democratic quality				
Not free (low)	–0.51***	–0.40	–0.36	–0.44*
	(0.10)	(0.25)	(0.38)	(0.23)
Partially free (medium)	–0.06	0.06	0.09	0.02
	(0.09)	(0.19)	(0.19)	(0.18)
Constant	5.2	5.91	6.51	6.18
	(0.43)	(0.94)	(2.04)	(1.12)
Period fixed effects	None	Yes	Yes	Yes
Number of recipients	104	104	102	104
Number of observations	5,529	5,529	5,429	5,529

SOURCES: Author's estimations using data from IMF (2006), Freedom House (2009), Gartzke (2010), World Bank (2010), and OECD, Development Database on Aid Activities: CRS Online (various years).

NOTES: Standard errors are in parentheses. An empty cell indicates that the corresponding variable is not included in the model. Log means a variable is in logarithmic form. RET: random-effects tobit. All RET model specifications include donor and recipient fixed effects. Observations are five-year averages during the 1973–2002 horizon. * indicates significant at the 10 percent level; ** indicates significant at the 5 percent level; *** indicates significant at the 1 percent level.

positive influence on aid eligibility. These results are consistent with the past studies and theoretical model of aid allocation discussed earlier. The coefficients for a failed-state dummy, political similarity, and US military grants are not robust to changes in model specification and estimation techniques. This indicates that failed-state status, political similarity, and US military grants are not significant in donors' determination of the eligibility of developing countries for foreign aid.

Aggregate Aid Allocation

At the aggregate aid allocation stage, estimated models have a good fit and explain about 60 to 70 percent of the variations in per capita aid commitments. Similar to what we see with regard to the eligibility stage, the estimated results suggest (Table 4.2) that the democratic quality of governance has a significant positive effect on the amount of per capita aid flows (commitments). At the margin, nondemocracies receive about 0.73–0.95 percent or $0.48–$0.62 less per capita aid than democracies. Similar results, but with smaller magnitude, can be observed with respect to partially free countries. In contrast to the eligibility stage, the coefficient for institutional quality of governance is insignificant.

The results also suggest that, much as at the eligibility stage, recipients' needs play a positive and significant role in donors' aid allocation decisions. The estimated coefficients for variables related to recipients' needs (income per capita and life expectancy) are significant across all estimated models. For example, a 1 percent change in GDP per capita is associated with a shift of 0.77–1.1 percent in per capita aid commitments, depending on the model specification. Similarly, a one-year change in life expectancy is associated with a change of about 1–3 percent in per capita aid commitments. Concerning the donors' interests (trade links and political similarities), only trade links have a significant positive association with per capita aid commitments. On average, a 1 percent increase in exports from a donor country to a recipient country is associated with an increase of about 0.5–0.8 percent in per capita aid commitments.

Besides, the estimates show that there is a systematic bias with respect to population size, which is consistent with past studies. More populous countries receive less aid in per capita terms. Further, previous studies on aid allocation suggested that the bandwagon effect has a significant positive association with per capita aid commitments. The elasticity of per capita aid commitments with respect to per capita aid received from other donors varies from 0.4 to 0.8 depending on the specification of the model. The results suggest that failed-state status has no significant impact on per capita aggregate aid commitments. Surprisingly, political similarities between donors and recipients have a significant negative impact on per capita aid disbursements.

Sectoral Allocation

Tables 4.3–4.5 provide the results of the three sectoral aid allocation models. Analysis of these results with respect to the quality of governance suggests that democratic quality of governance has a statistically significant positive impact on per capita aid commitments to the production and social sectors, but its impact on per capita aid to economic infrastructure is insignificant. Other things being equal, nondemocracies receive about 0.5 percent less aid per capita to the social sector (Table 4.3) and about 0.25 percent less aid per capita to the production sectors (Table 4.4) than do democracies. However, the results show no significant difference between the three groups of countries with respect to per capita aid commitments to economic infrastructure (Table 4.5). The results also show no considerable differences between partially free and democratic countries with respect to any categories of aid. Besides, the institutional quality of governance seems to have no significant impact on the sectoral allocation of aid.

The effects of variables that control for donors' interests and recipients' needs on per capita sectoral aid flows are similar to those found in the aggregate aid allocation equation. The failed-state dummy has a significant negative effect on per capita aid commitments to the production sectors. On average, failed states receive about 0.12 percent less aid per capita to the production sectors than do other countries.

Overall, the results show that donors' aid allocation decisions are considerably affected by both donors' own interests and recipients' needs at the eligibility and aid allocation stages. Also interesting are the results concerning the quality of governance. The results suggest that the better the quality of governance in a country, the higher the probability of its being eligible for foreign aid. The countries with better democratic governance also receive more aid per capita at the aggregate level. They also seem to receive relatively higher amounts of aid per capita for their production sectors and for social infrastructure at the margin. The results also suggest that donor and recipient fixed effects are statistically significant in both the aid eligibility and aid allocation stages. These findings indicate that there could be some important differences among various individual donors' aid allocation policies. For example, donors may pay special attention to their historical relationships with recipient countries in making aid allocation decisions. In the following chapter, such differences in donors' aid allocation policies will be further examined while constructing complicated instruments for aid components.

5 Aid and Economic Growth

One of the most enduring policy debates in development economics has to do with whether foreign aid helps recipient countries grow. This chapter contributes to this debate in three ways. First, most studies examine whether there is a causal link between aggregate aid flows and growth rates in aid recipient countries. However, as mentioned elsewhere, this approach might be flawed by the notion that aid flows are allocated to different sectors of the economy and for different purposes, and therefore they are less likely to affect growth in the same way and uniformly. This study disaggregates aggregate aid into sectoral aid flows using the OECD DAC classification and then estimates the impact of sectoral aid flows on economic growth. Second, the study examines whether the interaction of foreign aid with the quality of governance is important for the effectiveness of aid. Third, in examining the impact of foreign aid on economic growth, the study improves on and extends the most recent instrumentation strategy used in the aid effectiveness literature.

Analytical Framework

Figure 5.1 provides a heuristic diagram of the disaggregated aid flows and the potential channels of their impact on economic growth. The hypotheses to be tested within this framework are as follows. First, economic aid, which includes aid to the production sectors and aid to economic infrastructure, can affect economic growth by enlarging the pool of resources available for domestic investment. If economic aid supplements domestic resources, the impact of this sectoral aid flow on domestic investment should be positive. However, if it substitutes for domestic resources rather than supplementing them, its impact could be negligible or even negative. There are two plausible reasons that aid flows might substitute for domestic resources: (1) because aid flows are similar to public investment, they may crowd out private investment, and (2) because a recipient government is able to replace its own public investment expenditures with foreign aid. The coefficient of the ratio of economic aid to GDP in a cross-country investment regression could be equal to one if all economic aid

FIGURE 5.1 Outline of transmission channels in the aid–growth relationship

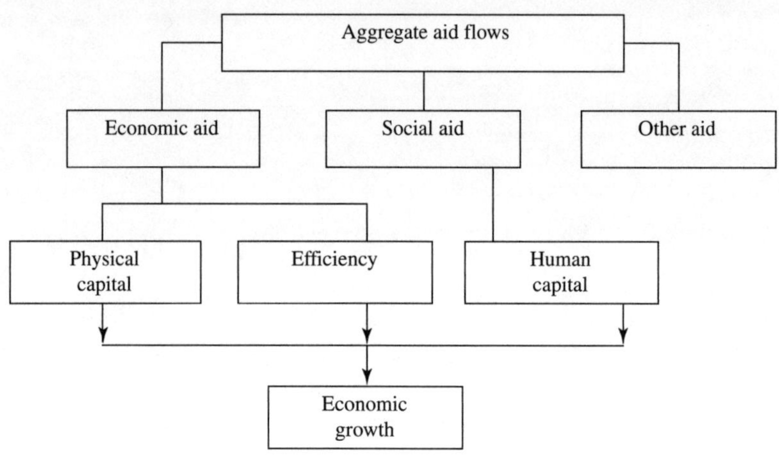

SOURCE: Author.

were usefully invested. However, this coefficient could be less than one if part of the economic aid were wasted or diverted for consumption purposes. Further, if the public investment financed by aid had spillover effects, in the long run it might reduce the cost of capital and therefore increase the demand for investment. In this case, the long-term impact of economic aid on investment could be greater than one.

In addition, the part of economic aid that goes to economic infrastructure might affect growth by improving the total productivity of the economy. This might happen if improvements in public infrastructure reduced the transaction costs of production in the private sector. For example, a reduction of communication costs can make international knowledge more accessible to local businesses and other establishments. Therefore, it seems plausible that countries with better infrastructure will have easier and cheaper access to knowledge stocks, which in turn should lead to higher rates of total productivity growth. Or the construction of new roads might reduce transaction costs, which in turn could improve the overall efficiency of the economy. However, empirical evidence suggests that in developing countries economic growth is primarily input driven; that is, capital accumulation, the use of additional labor, and total factor productivity increases are negligible (Krugman 1994; Young 1995; Collins and Bosworth 1996).

Further, aid to the social sector is intended to improve human capital and living standards in recipient countries, for example, by supporting public education or primary healthcare. Therefore, it is expected that this portion of aid may affect economic growth by creating additional human capital. In addition, the magnitude and direction of the previously mentioned impact channels of foreign aid on economic growth could be affected by the quality of governance in a given recipient country. On the one hand, the literature argues that foreign aid may be positively associated with economic growth and quality of life in democracies but detrimental in autocracies (Svensson 2000a; Kosack 2003). On the other hand, the literature also argues that democracies are inclined toward current expenditures and social programs because they are unable to ignore immediate public demands (Kosack 2003). This study examines whether the quality of democratic governance is a significant factor in aid effectiveness by allowing the measures of democratic governance to interact with sectoral aid components. As mentioned earlier, the measure of democratic governance used in this study is a combination of the political rights and civil liberties indicators of Freedom House. To account for possible nonlinearities in aid, democratic governance, and economic development, the study explores the interaction effects of sectoral aid components with three types of political governance: free, partially free, and not free.

The previously discussed framework leads us to the three main equations of the empirical model, which can be specified using the neoclassical growth framework augmented with human capital (Mankiw, Romer, and Weil 1992; Bassanini and Scarpetta 2001; Bassanini, Scarpetta, and Hemmings 2001). These three equations are for (1) real per capita income growth, (2) gross capital formation or investment, and (3) human capital.[1]

The per capita output equation is assumed to take the following form:

$$y = f(k, h, X), \tag{5.1}$$

where y is real per capita gross domestic product, k denotes the capital labor ratio, h is human capital, and X denotes the set of variables that may affect real per capita GDP. The latter may include inflation, trade openness, and financial depth, which further augment the neoclassical growth model with human capital. Further, following previous empirical literature on economic growth, it is also assumed that the quality of governance and foreign aid affect per capita economic growth. Hence, the following equation describes the growth (g) of real per capita GDP:

$$g = f(s_k, h, Gov, X_g, IAID), \tag{5.2}$$

where s_k is the net investment (incremental capital); h denotes human capital; Gov and $IAID$ denote governance and aid to economic infrastructure, respectively; and X_g refers to other control variables. The key parameters of interest in this equation measure the change in growth with respect to change (1) in the ratio of investment to GDP, (2) in human capital (for example, schooling), and (3) in the ratio of infrastructure aid to GDP. It is assumed that the first two are

1. The specifications of these equations are based on Bassanini and Scarpetta (2001); Bassanini, Scarpetta, and Hemmings (2001); and Baldacci et al. (2004). For details see Appendix D.

affected by economic and social aid, respectively. Following the aid effectiveness literature, the following variables may be included in X_g: initial level of per capita income, institutional quality, initial openness, inflation, financial depth measured as the ratio of broad money supply to GDP, initial coastal population density, malaria risk, ethnic fractionalization, geography, revolutions, and so forth. Additionally, there could be interactions between governance and the ratio of aid to GDP.

Similarly, the investment equation is identified as follows:

$$s_k = f(Gov, EAID, X_e), \tag{5.3}$$

where *EAID* denotes economic aid, which combines aid to the production sectors and economic infrastructure, and X_e refers to other control variables. The key parameter of interest in this equation measures the change in the ratio of investment to GDP with respect to the change in the ratio of economic aid to GDP. In specifying the control variables included in X_e, the study benefited from Fischer (1993), Mauro (1996), and Baldacci et al. (2004). These variables include inflation, initial level of policy and trade openness, financial depth, the ratio of FDI to GDP, and revolutions. These variables can influence the investment ratio by different channels. For example, financial depth can affect investment by improving the allocative efficiency of limited financial resources, lowering the cost of intermediation, and increasing the returns to investment (Agenor and Montiel 1996). Further, there could be interactions between governance and economic aid.

The impact of social aid on human capital is examined by using the following equation:

$$h = f(Gov, SAID, X_h), \tag{5.4}$$

where *SAID* denotes social aid and X_h refers to other control variables. The key parameter of interest in this equation measures the change in human capital with respect to the change in the ratio of social aid to GDP. Data limitations with respect to human capital outcome variables in developing countries are well known (Bennell 2002; Dreber, Nunnenkamp, and Thiele 2008). Human capital is approximated by secondary school enrollment under the assumption that greater enrollment ratios lead to greater human capital, which should be positively related to economic growth. For control variables, the study closely follows the literature on human capital and the education production function (for example, Baldacci et al. 2004; Dreber, Nunnenkamp, and Thiele 2008). Therefore, X_h may include the following variables: per capita income, initial level of schooling, infant mortality, fertility, the share of the population that is urban, the share of the population under age 15, and the ratio of public education expenditures to GDP. In addition, I include the malaria risk in the 1960s as an additional control for possible interactions of schooling with health capital. Alternative specifications also include the interactions of governance and social aid variables.

Overall, this framework differentiates three possible impact channels in the aid–growth relationship. First, it assumes that the impact of economic aid, which includes ODA to the production and economic infrastructure sectors, on economic growth arises from its impact on domestic investment (capital accumulation). Second, the part of economic aid that goes to economic infrastructure may directly impact economic growth by creating and improving the infrastructure (for example, roads), which helps to reduce transaction costs. Third, social aid, which includes ODA to the education and health sectors, may affect economic growth by building additional human capital.

Econometric Estimation Issues

Estimates of the three main equations—for economic growth, investment, and human capital—can be obtained using pooled cross-section or panel data regression methods. Cross-section regressions allow us to examine the long-run relationship among aid components and outcome variables. The most basic estimates of cross-sectional regressions can be obtained by using the standard OLS method. However, one cannot consider the OLS estimates evidence of a causal relationship between the key independent variable and the outcome if the error term is correlated with explanatory variables. The explanatory variables may be correlated with the error term in various circumstances. It is widely recognized that the relationship between foreign aid and growth (or income per capita) is endogenous and can be interpreted in two ways (Rajan and Subramanian 2008). For example, if countries tend to receive more aid because they are poor or because their socioeconomic conditions are deteriorating, the estimated coefficient would be biased toward zero and underestimate the impact of foreign aid. In the same way, if countries tend to receive less aid as their socioeconomic conditions improve, the estimated coefficient would be biased upward and overestimate the impact of foreign aid. Further, it is often argued that governance (democracy) is endogenous with respect to development (Barro 1996; Mobarak 2005). For instance, shocks to economic growth and income may well carry implications for the stability of governance structures, as well as the amount and sectoral allocation of aid flows, and vice versa. Another common reason for the violation of the zero conditional mean assumption is a classical measurement error in explanatory variables. If the explanatory variables are systematically measured with significant error, the unobserved error term in the relationship of interest will contain the measurement error. This error will be correlated with independent variables (Wooldridge 2002; Arellano 2003).

These problems are well recognized in the literature. One common method used to address issues of endogeneity in cross-sectional analysis is the IV approach. A relevant IV feature is that it needs further information in addition to that specified by the classical linear regression model. In particular, the IV estimator requires a valid instrument. To be a valid instrument it must be correlated with a key independent variable IV and uncorrelated with the model's error term. This study uses instrumentation with respect to two key independent variables, foreign aid and governance (details follow). Further, assuming that there is no correlation among the error terms of the three (growth, investment, and human capital) equations, single-equation IV estimations will produce unbiased and consistent estimates of the parameters of interest. However, apart from issues of endogeneity among aid, governance, and growth, some variables are jointly determined in our framework. On the one hand, the ratios of investment to GDP and secondary school enrollment are dependent variables in Equations 5.3 and 5.4, respectively. On the other hand, they are among the explanatory variables in the growth equation. This is more likely to create endogeneity between these variables and economic growth. Moreover, several right-hand-side variables are included in all three equations. As a result, the endogenous variables will be correlated with the error term, and the error terms among these three equations will also be correlated. Therefore, single-equation IV estimates could still be biased and inconsistent.

To cope with these issues, I solve these three equations in a simultaneous equations framework using the three-stage least-squares (3SLS) estimator. This method allows for endogenous variables to be among the right-hand-side variables in the main (growth) equation. In this way I estimate a system of structural equations that includes instrumentation for aid components at the first stage, investment and schooling at the second (intermediate) stage, and the growth equation at the third stage. The estimated investment equation and schooling equation serve as intermediate outcomes whose predicted values are used to replace the investment ratio and (contemporaneous) schooling in the per capita GDP growth equation. Therefore, it will be possible to claim that disaggregated aid has an effect on economic growth. Moreover, this method corrects for the correlation between the error term and the endogenous variables (aid components, investment, and schooling), as well as for the correlation among the error terms of the equations.

Another problem frequently encountered in analyzing the impact of aid on economic growth using cross-sectional data relates to outliers, values of the dependent variable that are abnormal given the values of the explanatory variables (response outliers) or odd values of the explanatory variables (design outliers). One way of dealing with outliers is merely to exclude them. However, this can substantially alter the results of empirical analysis. Another way of solving the problem could be to re-estimate the model iteratively omitting one observation at a time to see what exerts a significant influence on the set of estimates. I have chosen regressions with robust standard errors to address the problems related to outliers. The advantage of the robust estimation procedure is that it minimizes the influence of extreme observations on the estimated equation rather than omitting them. It uses the Huber-White sandwich estimator of variance in place of the traditional calculation. This alternative variance estimator produces consistent standard errors even if the data are weighted or the residuals are not identically distributed.

Apart from concerns about endogeneity and measurement error, the most common source of bias and inconsistency is unobserved heterogeneity or omitted (third) variable bias. Overall, the literature suggests that more than 50 variables are considerably correlated with growth (Levine and Renelt 1992). One may include them in the model whenever these variables are available. However, many of these variables are not readily available across countries. Moreover, some of these variables are not observed. For example, the literature suggests that country-specific unobservable factors, such as cultural factors, can affect both growth and exploratory variables simultaneously. This has potentially serious consequences if explanatory variables are correlated with those unobservable variables, whereas in a regression model regressors and unobservables are uncorrelated by construction. If those correlations between observables and unobservables are not zero, it renders standard estimation subject to bias and inconsistency; that is, if unobservables that have a direct impact on both dependent and explanatory variables are omitted, the error term will be correlated with explanatory variables and the regression coefficients will be biased measures of the parameters of interest. This is the so-called classical omitted variable bias. Further, it is most likely that temporal events render standard OLS estimation subject to bias and inconsistency. For example, the debt crisis in the early 1980s extended to a number of developing countries and most likely affected both development outcomes and aid variables. And the collapse of socialism at the end of the 1980s and the early 1990s affected development outcomes and governance in former socialist countries. This also affected aid flows to not only transition countries but many other developing countries.

In cross-section regressions, one cannot control for all possible ways in which countries might differ. Similarly, cross-section regressions do not allow one to control for temporal events. This can be done by using panel data regressions, which have the virtue of addressing the problem of unobserved heterogeneity by incorporating country fixed effects. Country fixed effects control for unobserved country-specific and time-invariant factors. Similarly, time fixed effects can be introduced to control for universal (country-invariant) time trends. This produces the fixed-effects panel estimation, which is one of the most popular estimation tools in growth regressions (Islam 1995). This method assumes that the unobserved error term x_{jt} has a factor structure, including a zero-mean country-specific time-invariant component h_j, a zero-mean time-specific country-invariant component, a zero-mean random component n_{jt} independent of all other values of this random component, and country- and time-specific components, that is,

$$\gamma_{jt} = \eta_j + \mu_t + \nu_{jt}. \tag{5.5}$$

Some major concerns remain after controlling for country-specific heterogeneity and period-specific fixed effects. One concern is that the residual may include time-varying and country-specific factors that affect the dependent variable. If these time-varying, country-specific factors are correlated with foreign aid, estimated coefficients of interest will be biased. Second, panel data structures consist of repeated measurements on the same unit, the recipient, that are "pooled" with those of other units to provide a combination of longitudinal and cross-sectional information. Therefore, there is a strong possibility of the existence of autocorrelation within panels and of cross-sectional correlation or heteroskedasticity across panels. In most panel data, the error terms associated with successive observations of the same unit—the observations of Uganda in 1992–97 and in 1998–2002, for instance—are correlated with each other. Another possibility is that the economies of many developing countries are dominated by a limited number of commodities. Therefore, fluctuations in world commodity markets may produce similar effects for a number of countries. In general, estimates of models of this structure are inconsistent if one uses the simple OLS method because the explanatory lagged dependent variable is correlated with the autocorrelated error term. Finally, the presence of classical measurement error in foreign aid or its sectoral allocation would bias the fixed-effects estimates toward zero. Because fixed-effects models produce inconsistent and biased estimates, they are not estimated.

A method that addresses identification issues in the presence of a panel data structure is to estimate moment equations using the GMM. There are two types of panel GMM regressions: the difference GMM estimator attributed to Arellano and Bond (1991) and the system GMM estimator credited to Blundell and Bond (1998). In both GMM estimators, identification relies on first differencing and using lagged values of the endogenous variables as instruments. In the difference GMM, lagged levels are used to instrument for the differenced explanatory variables, whereas in the system GMM, lagged differences of endogenous variables are used as instruments in the level equation and lagged levels of endogenous variables are used as instruments in the first differenced equation. Both GMM estimators have some limitations. The difference GMM estimator suffers from problems associated with weak instruments because lagged levels are typically not highly correlated with their differenced counterparts. System GMM, by exploiting the additional moment conditions in the levels equation, provides dramatic improvement in the accuracy of the estimates when the dependent variable is persistent. However, the lagged differences of the explanatory variables are valid instruments for the level equation only if they are orthogonal to the country fixed effects. This study provides results using both methods.

Given the previous discussion, this study addresses the econometric estimation issues discussed earlier using IV, 3SLS, and panel GMM regression methods. I present my analysis of the aid–growth relationship in two parts, starting with the cross-section regressions. This first part includes three stages: (1) the standard OLS regressions, (2) single-equation IV regressions; and (3) a system of simultaneous equation regression results. The second part of the analysis reports the results of the dynamic panel GMM results. The definitions and sources of the variables used are provided in Appendix C.

Cross-Section OLS Regressions

The special feature of this study is that it examines the impact of disaggregated aid on economic growth. However, to make the link to the existing literature, I begin with replicating the standard growth–aid model presented by Rajan and Subramanian (2008). The results of different specifications of the cross-sectional OLS regressions of this model are presented in Table 5.1. The dependent variable is the average growth rate of per capita income (GDP) of a country over a thirty-year (1973–2002) period. The key IVs are the average ratio of official development assistance to GDP over that period and the democratic quality of governance. The sample includes all developing countries that received aid during the postwar period and for which data are available.

The important question is what other explanatory variables should be included in the model. The study follows the latest aid and growth literature, in particular Rajan and Subramanian (2008) and Arndt, Jones, and Tarp (2010), to make the results comparable to those in the related literature. The explanatory variables in the model include initial level of per capita income, institutional quality, geography, initial life expectancy, initial trade policy (openness), financial depth, initial inflation, ethnic fractionalization, and revolutions.

The results of the OLS regressions are qualitatively quite similar to the results of Rajan and Subramanian (2008). In all five specifications, the estimated aid coefficient is negative, but it is statistically significant at conventional levels in only two specifications. The magnitude in these models suggests that an increase of 1 percentage point in the ratio of aggregate aid to GDP is associated with a negative long-run growth rate of approximately 0.08 percent per year (see columns M2 and M3 in Table 5.1). In all specifications, the estimated democracy coefficient is statistically insignificant. The estimated coefficient of the interaction between the aggregate aid ratio and the democracy score is practically no different from zero. Likewise, the coefficients of the interactions of aid with partially free and not free country dummies are statistically insignificant.

The results of different specifications of cross-sectional growth regressions of the disaggregated aid flows are presented in Table 5.2. The dependent variable is the same as in the aggregate aid regression—the average growth rate of per capita income (GDP) of a country over the thirty-year period 1973–2002. However, the right-hand-side variables are somewhat different. The key independent variables are the average ratio of annual aid given to economic infrastructure in that country to GDP over that period and the democratic quality of

TABLE 5.1 Impact of aggregate aid on growth, OLS estimations (dependent variable: average annual growth of per capita GDP)

	M1	M2	M3	M4	M5
Aid/GDP ratio	–0.073	–0.092	–0.079	–0.057	–0.094
	(0.047)	(0.038)**	(0.040)**	(0.042)	(0.044)
Governance	0.289	0.195	–0.006	0.302	0.259
	(0.152)*	(0.158)	(0.240)	(0.176)*	(0.198)
Aid/GDP ratio × governance		–0.032	–0.040		
		(0.020)	(0.025)		
Aid/GDP ratio × partially free				–0.069	–0.053
				(0.051)	(0.064)
Aid/GDP ratio × not free				–0.007	0.050
				(0.043)	(0.050)
Initial GDP per capita (log)	–1.368	–1.421	–1.530	–1.347	–1.494
	(0.304)***	(0.308)***	(0.346)***	(0.280)***	(0.302)***
Initial policy	0.796	0.696		0.759	
	(0.552)	(0.587)		(0.544)	
Institutional quality			0.561		0.507
			(0.205)***		(0.229)**
Initial infant mortality (log)	–0.977	–0.766	–0.808	–0.955	–0.909
	(0.526)*	(0.581)	(0.546)	(0.475)**	(0.507)*

Geography (absolute latitude)	0.028	0.028	0.022	0.030	0.022
	(0.015)*	(0.015)*	(0.017)	(0.014)**	(0.016)
Initial financial depth	0.003	0.006	–0.007		–0.008
	(0.015)	(0.017)	(0.022)		(0.020)
Initial inflation (log)	–0.316	–0.341	–0.401	–0.355	–0.428
	(0.340)	(0.347)	(0.310)	(0.298)	(0.317)
Revolutions	–1.779	–1.998	–1.233	–1.881	–1.469
	(0.682)***	(0.723)***	(0.579)***	(0.664)***	(0.577)**
Ethnic fractionalization	–1.248	–1.164	–0.441	–1.288	–0.259
	(0.686)*	(0.687)*	(0.698)	(0.689)*	(0.701)
Constant	16.823	16.656	14.937	16.744	14.939
n	78	78	66	79	66
Test for interactions (*p*-value)		0.012	0.055	0.045	0.082
F-statistic (overall model)	22.70	17.96	28.66	22.63	24.41
R-squared	0.65	0.66	0.71	0.66	0.72

SOURCES: Author's estimations using data from Rose (2004); Sala-i-Martin, Doppelhofer, and Miller (2004); IMF (2006); Desmet, Ortuño-Ortin, and Wacziarg (2009); Freedom House (2009); Heston, Summers, and Aten (2009); World Bank (2010); and OECD, Development Database on Aid from DAC Members: DAC Online (various years).

NOTES: OLS: ordinary least squares. Robust standard errors are in parentheses. An empty cell indicates that the corresponding variable is not included in the model. Log means a variable is in logarithmic form. * indicates significant at the 10 percent level; ** indicates significant at the 5 percent level; *** indicates significant at the 1 percent level. All specifications control for East Asian and Sub-Saharan African regional fixed effects. Observations are averages for the 1973–2002 horizon.

TABLE 5.2 Impact of disaggregated aid on growth, OLS estimations (dependent variable: average annual growth of per capita GDP)

	M1	M2	M3	M4	M5
Infrastructure aid/GDP ratio	–0.294	–0.198	–0.408	–0.201	–0.297
	(0.267)	(0.266)	(0.258)	(0.274)	(0.242)
Governance	0.226	0.138	0.217	0.137	0.299
	(0.221)	(0.212)	(0.231)	(0.251)	(0.230)
Infrastructure aid/GDP ratio × governance			–0.113	–0.005	
			(0.175)	(0.218)	
Infrastructure aid/GDP ratio × partially free					–0.693
					(0.396)*
Infrastructure aid/GDP ratio × not free					–0.059
					(0.286)
Initial GDP per capita (log)	–1.510	–1.599	–1.572	–1.598	–1.754
	(0.419)***	(0.426)***	(0.415)***	(0.437)***	(0.426)***
Initial life expectancy	0.010	0.016	0.004	0.016	–0.003
	(0.029)	(0.030)	(0.031)	(0.031)	(0.030)
Initial school enrollment	0.023	0.021	0.022	0.021	0.026
	(0.009)**	(0.009)**	(0.009)**	(0.009)**	(0.010)***
Openness	0.113		0.329		0.659
	(0.876)		(0.895)		(0.759)
Institutional quality		0.493		0.493	
		(0.207)**		(0.210)**	

Investment ratio	0.056	0.044	0.054	0.044	0.058
	(0.024)**	(0.026)*	(0.024)**	(0.027)	(0.024)**
Average inflation	–0.010	–0.012	–0.009	–0.012	–0.007
	(0.011)	(0.009)	(0.010)	(0.010)	(0.011)
Geography (absolute latitude)	0.023	0.023	0.027	0.023	0.034
	(0.023)	(0.016)	(0.024)	(0.016)	(0.022)
Malaria risk in 1966	–0.592	–0.287	–0.542	–0.287	–0.603
	(0.564)	(0.635)	(0.549)	(0.638)	(0.518)
Revolutions	–1.355	–0.623	–1.333	–0.625	–1.024
	(0.731)*	(0.556)	(0.729)*	(0.562)	(0.615)
Constant	9.388	7.284	10.107	7.291	11.123
n	73	66	73	66	76
Test for interactions (p-value)			0.377	0.828	0.1818
F-statistic (overall model)	9.17	9.45	8.86	8.82	8.10
R-squared	0.58	0.63	0.59	0.63	0.63

SOURCES: Author's estimations using data from Rose (2004); Sala-i-Martin, Doppelhofer, and Miller (2004); IMF (2006); Desmet, Ortuño-Ortin, and Wacziarg (2009); Freedom House (2009); Heston, Summers, and Aten (2009); World Bank (2010); and OECD, Development Database on Aid Activities: CRS Online (various years).

NOTES: OLS: ordinary least squares. Robust standard errors are in parentheses. An empty cell indicates that the corresponding variable is not included in the model. * indicates significant at the 10 percent level; ** indicates significant at the 5 percent level; *** indicates significant at the 1 percent level. All specifications control for East Asian and Sub-Saharan African regional fixed effects. Observations are averages for the 1973–2002 horizon.

governance. This model includes two additional key explanatory variables, including investment ratio and initial level of schooling. As in the aggregate aid model, the other explanatory variables in the model include initial level of per capita income, institutional quality, geography, initial life expectancy, initial trade policy (openness), initial average inflation, and revolutions. This specification replaces ethnic fractionalization with malaria risk in the 1960s. This variable was first used in the aid–growth literature by Arndt, Jones, and Tarp (2010) and allows us to create an additional link to the human capital equation.

The estimated coefficients of the ratio of aid given to economic infrastructure to GDP are negative, but none of them are statistically significant. The estimated coefficients for the democracy variable and its interactions with the ratio of aid to economic infrastructure to GDP are statistically insignificant in all model specifications. The estimated coefficients for investment ratio and initial levels of schooling are positive and mainly statistically significant at conventional levels. The magnitude of the coefficient for investment ratio suggests that an increase of 1 percentage point in the ratio of investment to GDP is associated with the long-term growth rate of approximately 0.05 percent. Likewise, the magnitude of the coefficient for initial schooling suggests that an additional percentage point in initial secondary school enrollment is associated with an average annual growth rate that is 0.02 percentage point higher.

The OLS results of different specifications of cross-sectional regressions of the investment equation with economic aid are presented in Table 5.3. The dependent variable is the average ratio of investment to GDP of a country over the thirty years between 1973 and 2002. The key independent variables are the average annual ratio of economic aid (the sum of aid to the production sectors and economic infrastructure) to GDP over a given period and the democratic quality of governance. The other explanatory variables in the investment equation include initial level of per capita income, initial policy (openness), initial financial depth, the ratio of foreign direct investment to GDP, average initial inflation, and revolutions.

The estimated coefficients of economic aid are positive in all estimated model specifications and statistically significant at conventional levels in two specifications. The magnitude of the estimated coefficient suggests that an increase of 1 percentage point in the ratio of economic aid to GDP is correlated with an investment ratio that is approximately 1.4 percentage point higher per year over the long run (Model 2). This effect is greater than the effect of FDI on the investment ratio. The estimated democracy coefficient and its interactions with economic aid are positive but statistically insignificant at conventional levels. Further, the estimated coefficients for the interactions of economic aid with different levels of democratic governance indicate that economic aid positively influences the investment ratio in partially free (2.4 percent) and not free countries (1.7 percent), whereas this impact is positive but statistically insignificant for free countries.

TABLE 5.3 Impact of economic aid on investment, OLS estimations (dependent variable: average annual investment/GDP ratio)

	Model 1	Model 2	Model 3	Model 4
Economic aid/GDP ratio	1.595	1.381	1.637	
	(0.595)**	(0.536)**	(0.864)*	
Governance	0.553	0.671	0.600	0.854
	(0.833)	(0.804)	(0.994)	(0.884)
Economic aid/GDP ratio × governance			0.066	
			(0.546)	
Economic aid/GDP ratio × free				0.599
				(0.588)
Economic aid/GDP ratio × partially free				2.353
				(0.984)**
Economic aid/GDP ratio × not free				1.708
				(0.528)***
Initial GDP per capita (log)	3.765	2.903	3.831	3.942
	(1.114)**	(1.298)**	(1.278)**	(1.150)***
Initial level of policy (Sachs-Warner)	–0.123		–0.079	0.115
	(3.184)		(3.120)	(3.267)
Openness		0.040		
		(0.021)*		
Initial financial depth	0.165	0.143	0.165	0.167
	(0.088)*	(0.072)*	(0.087)*	(0.090)*
Average inflation	–0.047	–0.019	–0.046	–0.058
	(0.032)	(0.034)	(0.032)	(0.032)
FDI/GDP ratio	0.949	0.568	0.938	0.785
	(0.409)**	(0.290)**	(0.399)**	(0.374)**
Revolutions	–6.791	–4.962	–6.683	–6.291
	(2.867)	(3.106)	(2.831)**	(3.005)**
Constant	–17.236	–12.752	–17.974	–19.966
n	81	81	81	81
Test for interactions (p-value)			0.020	0.034
F-statistic (overall model)	21.06	19.01	20.03	21.69
R-squared	0.68	0.69	0.68	0.70

SOURCES: Author's estimations using data from Rose (2004); Sala-i-Martin, Doppelhofer, and Miller (2004); IMF (2006); Desmet, Ortuño-Ortin, and Wacziarg (2009); Freedom House (2009); Heston, Summers, and Aten (2009); World Bank (2010); and OECD, Development Database on Aid Activities: CRS Online (various years).

NOTES: OLS: ordinary least squares; FDI: foreign direct investment. Robust standard errors are in parentheses. An empty cell indicates that the corresponding variable is not included in the model. Log means a variable is in logarithmic form. * indicates significant at the 10 percent level; ** indicates significant at the 5 percent level; *** indicates significant at the 1 percent level. All specifications control for East Asian and Sub-Saharan African regional fixed effects. Observations are averages for the 1973–2002 horizon.

Finally, the OLS estimates of cross-sectional regressions of the human capital equation with social aid are provided in Table 5.4. The dependent variable is the average secondary school enrollment in a given country, which is bounded by a lower bound of zero and an upper bound of 100.[2] Average years of schooling and primary school enrollment were also considered dependent variables. The key independent variables are the average ratio of annual social aid to GDP over 1973–2002 and the democratic quality of governance. The other explanatory variables in the human capital equation include initial level of per capita income, initial level of schooling, initial infant mortality, public expenditures in education, malaria risk in 1960s, average fertility, and share of the population under age 15.

The estimated coefficients of social aid are mainly positive but statistically insignificant in all specifications. The estimated coefficients for the democracy variable and its interactions with the ratio of social aid to GDP are statistically insignificant at conventional levels. The estimates reveal a considerable degree of inertia in secondary school enrollment. Among other explanatory variables, initial per capita income, average fertility, and malaria risk in the 1960s are both statistically and practically significant. However, as Rajan and Subramanian mention, "one cannot take these estimates seriously as evidence of causality because of the problem of endogeneity" (2008, 647). This problem is well recognized in the aid effectiveness literature. As discussed earlier, one possible solution to this problem is instrumentation.

An Instrumentation Strategy

Instrument for Aid

The aid effectiveness literature uses various instruments to tackle the endogeneity between aid and growth. Rajan and Subramanian provide a brief overview of the instrument sets used in this literature and discuss the limitations of these instruments. Then they provide a conceptually different instrumentation strategy, exploiting the fact that aid is often extended for noneconomic reasons; their "key idea for instrumentation is to model the supply of aid based on donor-related rather than recipient-specific characteristics" (2008, 648). Their complicated instrument for aid takes into account history and influence factors. The historic relationships between donors and recipients are captured by colonial links and commonality of language traits. Influence is proxied by the ratio of the donor population to that of the recipient. The construction of the instrument

---

2. As Dreber, Nunnenkamp, and Thiele suggested, "the upper bound may lead to biased results in the sense that aid can have little effect on enrollment in recipient countries with enrollment rates close to 100 percent" (2008, 297–298). I estimated alternative specifications of the schooling regression by using the logarithm of school enrollment as dependent variable but the results would not change considerably.

TABLE 5.4 Impact of social aid on schooling, OLS estimations (dependent variable: secondary school enrollment)

	Model 1	Model 2	Model 3	Model 4
Social aid/GDP ratio	–0.121	0.899	2.882	2.738
	(0.748)	(0.961)	(1.780)	(1.944)
Governance	–0.311	0.051	–1.019	–0.754
	(1.880)	(1.813)	(1.783)	(1.820)
Social aid/GDP ratio × governance		1.328		
		(0.813)		
Social aid/GDP ratio × partially free			–3.629	–3.458
			(2.081)	(2.237)
Social aid/GDP ratio × not free			–3.006	–3.031
			(2.035)	(2.220)
Initial secondary enrollment	0.764	0.765	0.773	0.716
	(0.159)***	(0.158)***	(0.160)***	(0.159)***
Initial GDP per capita (log)	8.456	9.007	9.127	9.013
	(2.556)***	(2.481)***	(2.571)***	(2.580)***
Infant mortality (log)	7.023	7.017	7.331	6.697
	(3.542)*	(3.516)**	(3.553)**	(3.325)*
Average fertility	–8.975	–9.716	–8.964	–6.446
	(2.550)***	(2.778)***	(2.521)***	(2.169)***
Malaria risk in 1966	–10.630	–10.051	–11.770	–12.865
	(4.523)**	(4.682)**	(4.789)**	(5.183)**
Education expenditures (percent of GDP)	–0.787	–1.120	–0.971	–0.399
	(1.074)	(1.096)	(1.155)	(1.172)
Population under 15 (percent)	0.818	0.828	0.854	
	(0.447)*	(0.443)*	(0.463)*	
Constant	–47.019	–49.264	–51.975	–24.019
n	76	76	76	76
Test for interactions (*p*-value)		0.402	0.452	0.575
F-statistic (overall model)	56.7	58.7	51.2	59.0
R-squared	0.86	0.87	0.87	0.86

SOURCES: Author's estimations using data from Rose (2004); Sala-i-Martin, Doppelhofer, and Miller (2004); IMF (2006); Desmet, Ortuño-Ortin, and Wacziarg (2009); Freedom House (2009); Heston, Summers, and Aten (2009); World Bank (2010); and OECD, Development Database on Aid Activities: CRS Online (various years).

NOTES: OLS: ordinary least squares. Robust standard errors are in parentheses. An empty cell indicates that the corresponding variable is not included in the model. Log means a variable is in logarithmic form. * indicates significant at the 10 percent level; ** indicates significant at the 5 percent level; *** indicates significant at the 1 percent level. All specifications control for East Asian and Sub-Saharan African regional fixed effects. Observations are averages for the 1973–2002 horizon.

starts from the donor–recipient relationships and aggregates up, in contrast to the literature that chooses the instrument at the recipient country level.[3]

The instrumentation strategy of Rajan and Subramanian (2008) is compelling, but there are two important weaknesses. First, it was argued that this complicated instrument includes little information beyond the recipients' population size. Bazzi and Clemens (2009) claim that, for the period 1970–2000, the instrument they constructed is almost perfectly correlated with the log of recipients' population with a correlation coefficient of 0.93. Therefore, in reality Rajan and Subramanian's complicated instrument is indistinguishable from instrumenting exclusively with recipients' population size (Bazzi and Clemens 2009).

Second, the instrument constructed by Rajan and Subramanian (2008) is further weakened by the inclusion of colonizer dummies and their interactions with population ratios in its construction (Arndt, Jones, and Tarp 2010). This notion is supported by theoretical and empirical studies that show that a country's colonial past and the identity of the colonizer are significant determinants of subsequent economic development (Grier 1999; Acemoglu, Johnson, and Robinson 2001; Berthocchi and Canova 2002; Nunn 2007). For example, Acemoglu, Johnson, and Robinson (2001) find that in former colonies where the colonizer was focused mainly on extraction, weak property rights institutions were established and persist today. Berthocchi and Canova (2002) show that the peculiarities of past colonial experiences and the identity of the colonizer are important reasons for the subsequent rates of economic growth, the investment/output ratio, and school attainment in former colonies.

In what follows, this study improves on and modifies the instrumentation strategy suggested by Rajan and Subramanian (2008). The construction of an instrument for aid in this study follows their work and recognizes that most donors pay attention to historical and influence factors in their aid allocation decisions. As in the work of Rajan and Subramanian, historic relationships are captured through colonial links and commonality of language. Similarly, influence is proxied by the logarithm of the ratio of the donor population to the recipient population, assuming that the larger the donor is relative to the recipient, the more influence the donor is likely to have on the recipient. In addition, the interactions between relative size and colonial links, and between relative size and language traits, are included to capture the relational effects between history and influence factors.

The elements of the complicated instrument used in this study so far are the same as in Rajan and Subramanian (2008). However, now I make several important modifications in the elements of this complicated instrument. First, I drop colonizer-specific variables and their interactions except the dummy for

3. This approach is similar to that of Frankel and Romer (1999) in the trade-growth literature.

Portuguese colonies. The rationale for this is that Portugal is a very small donor and gives aid mainly to its former colonies. Second, following Arndt, Jones, and Tarp (2010), I include donor-specific fixed effects in the construction of the complicated instrument. This notion is supported by the findings of various aid allocation studies, such as Alesina and Dollar (2000) and Berthélemy (2006a, 2006b), and the results presented in Chapter 4 of this study. Third, I control for donors' political and strategic interests. The aid allocation literature (Alesina and Dollar 2000; Younas 2008) shows that political similarity between donors and recipients as measured by voting patterns in the UN is an important factor in the aid allocation decisions of many donors. Strategically oriented donors, such as the United States, are more likely to reward recipients with similar voting patterns in the UN. This impact is captured by including the interaction between political similarity and a strategic donor dummy. Based on the results of the aid allocation analysis in Chapter 4, Australia, New Zealand, the United Kingdom, and the United States are identified as strategic donors. Further, I assume that donors are more likely to reward larger recipients with more aid if they have similar political interests and voting patterns in the UN. This channel is captured by including the term of interaction between the relative size and political similarities variables.

Fourth, in addition to history and geopolitical factors, foreign aid has been associated with donors' trade promotion interests. For example, Barrett and Maxwell suggest that "the commodity composition of democratic donor countries' food aid reflects those items currently in surplus in the donor economy and the political power of particular commodity interest groups" (Barrett and Maxwell 2005, 32). This finding could be applicable to other components of foreign aid. To capture the effects of donor trade promotion and commercial interests, in this study I make a plausible assumption that, the more donors, especially smaller ones, expect to expand the export markets for their domestic companies, the more likely they are to want to give aid. These effects are captured by including the interaction between relative size and donors' exports. The expected sign for the interaction term is negative because donors would probably value their exports to relatively larger recipients.

Finally, to differentiate between social and economic aid, in this study I use some recipient-specific variables to construct instruments for these aid components. The initial (early 1970s) values of life expectancy, fertility, access to drinking water, and the ratio of physicians to the population are included in the construction of the instrument for social aid. The initial (early 1970s) share of agricultural value added in GDP and the initial share of rural residents in the total population are included in the economic aid equation. Donors' commercial interests seem more pronounced in the allocation of economic aid. That is why this variable is also included in the instrument for economic aid. Also, the dummy for a colony of Portugal is included in the instrument for economic aid but not that for social aid.

Adding these modifications, the decision regarding the allocation of aid by a donor (i) to a recipient (j) can be expressed by the following model:

$$\frac{A_{ij}}{GDP_{ij}} = \beta_0 + \beta_1 COMCOL_{ij} + + \beta_2 CURCOL_{ij} + \beta_3 COMLANG_{ij}$$
$$+ \beta_4 COLPOR_{ij} + \beta_5 \log(POP_i/POP_j) + \beta_6 \log(POP_i/POP_j) \times COMCOL_{ij}$$
$$+ \beta_7 \log(POP_i/POP_j) \times COLPOR_{ij} + \beta_8 POLSIM_{ij} + \beta_9 POLSIM_j$$
$$\times SD_i + \beta_{10} \log(POP_i/POP_j) \times POLSIM_{ij} + \beta_{11} \log(EXPORT_{ij})$$
$$+ \beta\beta_{12} \log(EXPORT_{ij}) \times \log(POP_i/POP_j) + \Sigma\beta_k X_{kj} + d_i + \varepsilon_{ij}, \qquad (5.6)$$

where A_{ij} is the aid given by donor i to recipient j. GDP_j is the recipient country's GDP. The first three explanatory variables capture historic factors: *COMCOL* is a dummy that takes a value of one if the recipient was ever a colony of the donor, *CURCOL* is a dummy that takes a value of one if the recipient was in a colonial relationship with the donor during the period captured in the study, and *COMLANG* is a dummy that takes a value of one if the donor and recipient share a common language. The variable *COLPOR* controls for colonial relationships with Portugal.

As in Rajan and Subramanian (2008), donor size relative to the recipient is measured by the ratio of the logarithm of the initial populations of donor and recipient ($\log(POP_i/POP_j)$). Donors' relative influence is additionally measured by the interaction of the relative population size and the colonial variables (*COMCOL* and *COLPOR*). *POLSIM* measures political similarities between the donor and the recipient using their voting patterns in the UN. *SD* is a dummy variable that takes a value of one if the donor is classified as a strategic donor. *EXPORT* controls for the donor's commercial interests measured by initial exports from the donor to the recipient.[4] For example, an increase of 1 percent in initial total donor exports is associated with an increase of 1.1 percent in the ratio of economic aid to GDP given by the average donor. X_{kj} is a matrix of recipient-specific variables, including the initial (1970) values of life expectancy, share of agriculture in GDP, share of rural people in the total population, fertility, access to drinking water, and the ratio of physicians to the population.[5]

The estimated equations are then aggregated across donors to yield a level of the fitted value of respective ratios of aid to GDP for the recipient for 1973–2002. Table 5.5 presents estimates of the model for aggregate aid (AA), social

4. To minimize endogeneity-related problems, the study uses the initial rather than the average value of donor exports.

5. Inclusion of these variables in the construction of instruments for economic and social aid raises endogeneity-related concerns. One may argue that these variables are predetermined but not completely exogenous to dependent variables. This concern is addressed later in the study by explicitly checking the exclusion restrictions for each of these variables.

aid (SSA), economic aid (ESA), and aid to economic infrastructure (ISA). Nearly all the right-hand-side variables are significant for all aid categories, and they account for reasonable shares (between 36 and 43 percent) of the variations in the donor aid allocation decision. Past colonial linkages seem more important for economic and aggregate aid than for the social aid component. On the contrary, more recent colonial linkages seem more important for social aid. Political similarities seem more important for so-called strategic donors, such as the United States. Donors' commercial interests seem quite important to donors in the allocation of economic aid. The measures of influence and its interactions with other variables are mostly significant for all aid categories. The larger the donor relative to the recipient, the greater the aid given, and this effect is magnified, as assumed, in cases in which the donor (1) had a colonial relationship with the recipient, (2) had a similar voting pattern in the UN (demonstrating political similarity), and (3) had an initial strong commercial interest in the recipient. The signs of these scale effects are mostly as expected.

TABLE 5.5 Estimation of exogenous variation in the allocation of aid by donors across recipients (dependent variable: aid/recipient GDP ratio)

	AA	SSA	ESA	ISA
Dummy for pairs that ever had a colonial relationship	0.289 (0.091)***	0.150 (0.039)***	0.229 (0.053)***	0.124 (0.029)***
Dummy for pairs that recently had a colonial relationship	0.494 (0.297)*	0.230 (0.056)***	–0.084 (0.076)	–0.030 (0.042)
Dummy for pairs that have a common language	0.090 (0.024)***	0.021 (0.018)	0.034 (0.024)	0.007 (0.013)
Dummy for a country that ever had a colonial relation with Portugal	0.272 (0.066)***		0.083 (0.037)***	0.047 (0.020)**
Ratio of population of donor relative to recipient (log)	0.103 (0.013)***	0.048 (0.007)***	0.094 (0.012)***	0.043 (0.007)***
Ratio of population of donor relative to recipient (log) × colony	0.021 (0.049)	–0.005 (0.014)	0.055 (0.020)***	0.019 (0.011)*
Ratio of population of donor relative to recipient (log) × Portugal colony	0.118 (0.027)***		0.085 (0.014)***	0.053 (0.008)***
Political similarity (affinity)	–0.075 (0.72)	–0.098 (0.095)	–0.184 (0.123)	–0.070 (0.068)
Ratio of population of donor relative to recipient (log) × political similarity	–0.150 (0.025)***	–0.066 (0.015)***	–0.114 (0.021)***	–0.049 (0.012)***

(*continued*)

TABLE 5.5 Continued

	AA	SSA	ESA	ISA
Political similarity × strategic donor	0.755 (0.268)***	0.609 (0.191)***	0.676 (0.258)***	0.305 (0.143)**
Initial donor exports to recipient country (log)	0.017 (0.006)***		0.011 (0.005)**	0.007 (0.003)***
Ratio of population of donor relative to recipient (log) × exports			0.009 (0.002)***	–0.004 (0.001)***
Initial life expectancy (1970) (log)	–0.452 (0.054)***	–0.322 (0.049)***		
Initial share of agriculture in GDP (1970), percent	0.003 (0.000)***		0.002 (0.001)***	0.001 (0.000)***
Initial share of rural population (1970), percent			0.001 (0.000)**	0.001 (0.000)**
Initial ratio of physicians to population (1970s)		0.041 (0.023)*		
Initial access to drinking water (1970s), percent		–0.0004 (0.0003)		
Initial fertility (1970s)		0.002 (0.005)		
Constant	1.707	1.330	–0.104	–0.068
n	3,486	1,820	1,820	1,820
F-statistic	40.7	25.4	24.1	19.5
R-squared	0.38	0.36	0.43	0.36

SOURCES: Author's estimations using data from Rose (2004); Sala-i-Martin, Doppelhofer, and Miller (2004); IMF (2006); Desmet, Ortuño-Ortin, and Wacziarg (2009); Freedom House (2009); Heston, Summers, and Aten (2009); World Bank (2010); and OECD, Development Database on Aid Activities: CRS Online (various years).

NOTES: AA: aggregate aid; SSA, ESA, and ISA: aid to the social, economic, and infrastructure sectors, respectively. All models include donor fixed effects. All standard errors are robust. An empty cell indicates that the corresponding variable is not included in the model. Log means a variable is in logarithmic form. Observations are averages for the 1973–2002 horizon. * indicates significant at the 10 percent level; ** indicates significant at the 5 percent level; *** indicates significant at the 1 percent level.

How much information about different components of aid is included in these complex instruments? The following analysis shows that the instruments previously described account for major parts of the variation in the aggregated and disaggregated aid categories. The relationship between actual and constructed aid ratios is strong, with correlation coefficients of about 0.7. Panels A, B, C, and D of Table 5.6 provide further tests of the quality of the constructed instruments (as in Frankel and Romer 1999). For example, as column 1 of Panel C in this table shows, a regression of the actual ratio of economic aid to GDP on a constant and constructed economic aid yields a coefficient on the con-

TABLE 5.6 The relationship between actual and constructed aid variables

	1	2	3
	Panel A: Aggregate aid		
Constant	0.150	17.209	–1.194
Constructed aggregate aid	0.993		0.986
	(0.045)***		(0.042)***
Log population		–2.210	–0.238
		(0.604)***	(0.382)
F-statistic	487.2	6.8	201.1
R-squared	0.79	0.14	0.80
	Panel B: Social aid		
Constant	–0.023	4.816	0.242
Constructed social aid	1.135		1.063
	(0.086)***		(0.143)***
Log population		–0.595	0.129
		(0.150)***	(0.129)
F-statistic	56.3	8.2	21.1
R-squared	0.64	0.17	0.64
	Panel C: Economic aid		
Constant	0.101	5.691	–0.227
Constructed economic aid	0.913		0.881
	(0.072)***		(0.072)***
Log population		–0.769	–0.251
		(0.203)***	(0.167)***
F-statistic	159.8	7.5	54.0
R-squared	0.59	0.16	0.61
	Panel D: Infrastructure aid		
Constant	0.049	2.790	–0.266
Constructed infrastructure aid	0.875		0.841
	(0.073)***		(0.074)***
Log population		–0.362	–0.129
		(0.093)***	(0.074)*
F-statistic	142.6	7.8	50.1
R-squared	0.61	0.16	0.63

SOURCES: Author's estimations using data from Heston, Summers, and Aten (2009); World Bank (2010); OECD, Development Database on Aid Activities: CRS Online (various years); and OECD, Development Database on Aid from DAC Members: DAC Online (various years).

NOTES: The dependent variables are the ratios of actual aid to GDP. The key independent variables are the respective ratios of constructed aid to GDP. All regressions control for land area. Robust standard errors are in parentheses. An empty cell indicates that the corresponding variable is not included in the model. Log means a variable is in logarithmic form. Observations are averages for the 1973–2002 horizon. * indicates significant at the 10 percent level; ** indicates significant at the 5 percent level; *** indicates significant at the 1 percent level.

structed economic aid of 0.913 and a *t*-statistic of 12.6. Similar observations can be made about other aid ratios looking at Panels A, B, and D of Table 5.6.

As shown in the previous chapter, however, per capita aid flows and country size (population) are negatively correlated: the larger a country is, the less aid it receives per capita. Therefore, if there is no control for size in aid effectiveness analysis, constructed aid may be negatively correlated with the residual and may become a weak instrument (as discussed by Bazzi and Clemens 2009). Intuitively, donors may want to give more aid to smaller countries simply because they might assume that it is easier to affect economic development in smaller countries. Therefore, the component of the constructed aid that is correlated with country size cannot be used to estimate aid's impact on development. The constructed aid ratios are in fact negatively correlated with country size. For instance, the correlation of the constructed instrument for aggregate aid with the logarithm of the recipients' initial population is about –0.4, which is significantly lower than the correlation of the constructed instrument from Rajan and Subramanian (2008). Similarly, a regression of the constructed aggregate aid on a constant and the country size yields negative and statistically significant coefficients on log population.

Therefore, in examining whether the constructed aid ratios provide useful information about the actual aid ratios, one needs to ask whether they provide information beyond that included in country size. For that reason, columns 2 and 3 of Table 5.6 compare the regressions of the actual aid ratios on the country size with regressions that also include the respective constructed aid ratios. As expected, country size has a negative effect on aid ratios. However, the coefficients of the respective constructed aid ratios change slightly when the country size (population) measures are added. For instance, as column 3 in Panel C of Table 5.6 shows, a regression of the economic aid ratio on a constant, the constructed economic aid ratio, and the log of initial population yields a coefficient on the constructed economic aid of 0.881 and a *t*-statistic of 12.2. This regression coefficient is slightly less than a coefficient obtained without controlling for the country size. Similar results are obtained concerning other aid ratios. The important message of Table 5.6 is that the constructed aid ratios provide a significant amount of information about actual aid ratios beyond country size, and they can be used as instrumental variables in respective aid effectiveness regressions.

Instrument for Democracy

The instrument for democracy (governance) proposed in this study is the level of constraints on the executive in 1900, coded from the Polity IV dataset (Marshall, Jaggers, and Gurr 2010).[6] This variable refers to the extent of institutional

6. This variable was used by Acemoglu, Johnson, and Robinson (2001) as an alternative instrument for institutions in their analysis of the effect of institutions on economic performance.

constraints on the decisionmaking powers of the executive branch, whether an individual or a collective executive. This is similar to the notion of "horizontal accountability" found in the democracy literature, but it assumes that dictators may also be bound by certain institutional constraints. The degree of checks and balances among the various parts of the government is coded on a 7-point scale that ranges from "unlimited executive authority" (1) to "executive parity or subordination" (7). Democratic governance is the end product of long-term political evolution. A variety of historical evidence indicates that the governance structures set up during the colonial era persisted and that the institutions of governance established during the early phases of colonialism have formed the basis of the current institutions in many countries (Acemoglu, Johnson, and Robinson 2001). That is why constraints on the executive in 1900 were expected to be correlated with the quality of current democratic governance in a given country. In the first-stage democracy regressions, the constraints on the executive in 1900 remain highly significant even after controlling for an indicator for independence after 1945.

Specification 1 in Table 5.7 presents the first-stage regression of the democracy index, where constraints on the executive in 1900 and an indicator for countries that gained independence after 1945 are used as instruments. The F-statistic for the joint significance of excluded instruments is very high (17.1), with a p-value of 0.0000. The variable constraint on the executive in 1900 has a high t-statistic and is significant at the 1 percent level.

Specifications 2 and 3 in Table 5.7 reflect alternative first-stage regressions where an indicator of a majority Muslim population (as in Mobarak 2005) and the historical European settler mortality estimate from Acemoglu, Johnson, and Robinson (2001) are used as alternative instruments for democracy. However, the first-stage regressions (Table 5.7) indicate that the Muslim indicator and European settler mortality do not identify democracy as well as constraints on the executive.

Aid and Growth: Cross-Section IV Results

This section reports the results of cross-country single-equation IV results. For each category of aid, first, it examines whether instrumentation for aid and for democracy affects aid effectiveness. I provide three alternative estimations. The first estimation is obtained by using the two-stage least-squares (2SLS) estimator. If the instruments are weakened for obvious reasons, the 2SLS estimates can be misleading. The potential sources of weakening of the constructed instruments for different aid categories are variables (for example, population ratio) included in the instrumentation framework (Equation 5.6). That is why I also estimate the effects of aid using the limited-information, maximum-likelihood (LIML) estimator, which is more robust to weak instruments than the 2SLS. Besides, as an additional robustness check I report the estimates obtained by

TABLE 5.7 First-stage regression of instruments for governance (dependent variable: democracy index)

	1	2	3
Constraints on executives in 1900	0.271		
	(0.051)***		
Indicator for countries that gained independence after 1945	–0.882		
	(0.243)***		
Indicator for countries with Muslim majority populations		–0.660	
		(0.314)**	
Estimate of European settlers in 1900			0.017
			(0.014)
Aid/GDP ratio	–0.000	–0.004	0.001
	(0.030)	(0.038)	(0.035)
Aid/GDP ratio fitted	0.022	0.027	0.022
	(0.029)	(0.036)	(0.034)
Initial GDP per capita (log)	0.567	0.399	0.390
	(0.251)**	(0.286)	(0.317)
Initial level of policy (Sachs-Warner)	0.617	1.140	1.109
	(0.325)*	(0.365)***	(0.420)**
Initial infant mortality (log)	–0.284	–0.730	–0.785
	(0.351)	(0.452)	(0.456)*
Geography (absolute latitude)	0.004	0.005	0.005
	(0.012)	(0.014)	(0.015)
Initial financial depth	–0.022	–0.020	–0.025
	(0.010)**	(0.013)	(0.017)
Initial inflation (log)	0.012	–0.138	–0.295
	(0.190)	(0.170)	(0.216)
Revolutions	–0.813	0.129	–0.022
	(0.522)	(0.575)	(0.631)
Ethnic fractionalization	0.144	–0.272	–0.547
	(0.516)	(0.693)	(0.723)
Constant	0.900	5.086	5.892
n	79	80	79
F-test of excluded instruments	17.08	4.41	1.51
Probability > *F*	0.000	0.040	0.224
F-statistic (overall model)	13.16	8.51	8.68
R-squared	0.67	0.54	0.51

SOURCES: Author's estimations using data from Rose (2004); Sala-i-Martin, Doppelhofer, and Miller (2004); Desmet, Ortuño-Ortin, and Wacziarg (2009); Heston, Summers, and Aten (2009); Marshall, Jaggers, and Gurr (2010); World Bank (2010); and OECD, Development Database on Aid from DAC Members: DAC Online (various years).

NOTES: Robust standard errors are in parentheses. An empty cell indicates that the corresponding variable is not included in the model. Log means a variable is in logarithmic form. * indicates significant at the 10 percent level; ** indicates significant at the 5 percent level; *** indicates significant at the 1 percent level.

using Fuller's modified LIML estimator. Finally, I check whether the instruments satisfy the exclusion restrictions and pass overidentification tests.

Aggregate Aid

Panel A of Table 5.8 reports the second stage of the aggregate aid IV specifications. Column 1 of the table reports regression results using the 2SLS estimator. The next two columns introduce the LIML and Fuller's modified LIML estimators. The equations are well specified, and the instrumentation is very strong, as indicated by the Angrist and Pischke (2009) (AP) chi-squared and *F*-statistics.[7] In the first-stage regression results (Panel B), the AP chi-squared underidentification test readily rejects their null hypothesis at conventional levels, suggesting that the instrument is adequate to identify the equation. Likewise, the AP *F*-test for excluded instruments suggests that the constructed instrument for the ratio of aggregate aid to GDP is very strong. Not surprisingly, the LIML estimates are virtually identical and the Fuller estimates are almost identical to the 2SLS results. The overidentification restrictions are not rejected at conventional levels of significance, as proved by the Hansen *J*-statistic. The coefficient for the aggregate aid ratio is not statistically different from zero in all specifications. The coefficient for the democracy score is also statistically insignificant at conventional levels. The estimated coefficients of the interaction of democracy with aggregate aid suggest that the effect of this interaction is virtually zero (columns Inter1 and Inter2). Overall, instrumentation seems to make the impact of aggregate aid on average per capita growth virtually zero. Concerning the possibility that the impact of aid on growth might depend on democratic governance, the level of democracy and its interaction with aid are neither individually nor jointly significant at conventional levels. Likewise, the interactions of aid with different types of democratic governance are statistically insignificant.

Table 5.9 provides a summary of the IV tests for the exclusion restrictions. In the instrumentation framework implemented earlier, the variables colony of Portugal, recipient population size, initial share of agriculture, initial donor exports, and initial life expectancy may be correlated with growth via channels other than the endogenous aid variable. For example, recipients' population size may affect their growth rates through various channels, including international and domestic trade (Frankel and Romer 1999; Deaton 2009). In this case, the exclusion restriction might be problematic.

7. When there are multiple endogenous regressors, conventional *F*-statistics are no longer appropriate (Angrist and Pischke 2009). In this study I deal with two endogenous regressors: aid and governance. Therefore, I use the AP first-stage chi-squared test as a test for underidentification and the AP first-stage *F*-test as a test for weak identification. In contrast to conventional *F*-tests (Cragg and Donald 1993; Kleibergen and Paap 2006), which test the identification of the equation as whole, the AP first-stage chi-squared and *F*-tests are tests of whether one of the endogenous regressors is underidentified or weakly identified.

TABLE 5.8 Impact of aggregate aid on growth, instrumental variable (IV) estimations

	IV-2SLS	IV-LIML	IV-Fuller	Inter1	Inter2
Panel A: IV estimations (dependent variable: average annual growth of per capita GDP)					
Aid/GDP ratio	–0.018	–0.018	–0.019	–0.025	0.072
	(0.034)	(0.034)	(0.034)	(0.049)	(0.089)
Governance	0.453	0.453	0.447	0.465	0.308
	(0.241)*	(0.242)*	(0.233)*	(0.291)	(0.347)
Aid/GDP ratio × governance				–0.008	
				(0.041)	
Aid/GDP ratio × partially free					–0.118
					(0.087)
Aid/GDP ratio × not free					–0.096
					(0.082)
Initial GDP per capita (log)	–1.201	–1.201	–1.204	–1.217	–1.139
	(0.373)***	(0.373)***	(0.369)***	(0.394)***	(0.395)***
Initial level of policy (Sachs-Warner)	0.611	0.611	0.620	0.579	0.674
	(0.565)	(0.565)	(0.561)	(0.719)	(0.642)
Initial infant mortality (log)	–1.031	–1.031	–1.035	–0.967	–1.144
	(0.523)**	(0.523)**	(0.521)**	(0.682)	(0.602)
Geography	0.044	0.044	0.043	0.044	0.047
	(0.015)***	(0.015)***	(0.015)***	(0.016)***	(0.016)***
Initial financial depth	0.002	0.002	0.002	0.003	–0.003
	(0.016)	(0.016)	(0.016)	(0.018)	(0.017)
Initial inflation (log)	–0.345	–0.345	–0.346	–0.364	–0.348
	(0.313)	(0.313)	(0.313)	(0.342)	(0.301)
Revolutions	–1.659	–1.659	–1.659	–1.673	–1.679
	(0.721)**	(0.721)**	(0.718)**	(0.766)**	(0.705)**

Ethnic fractionalization	–0.883	–0.882	–0.888	–0.872	–0.868
	(0.685)	(0.685)	(0.683)	(0.779)	(0.772)
Constant	14.456	14.452	14.537	14.286	15.111
Test for interactions (*p*-value)				0.440	0.540
F-statistic (overall model)	14.22	14.21	14.40	18.97	20.23
R-squared	0.63	0.63	0.63	0.62	0.64
Panel B: First-stage regression (dependent variable: total aid/GDP ratio)					
Fitted aid/GDP ratio	0.840	0.840	0.840	***	***
	(0.065)	(0.065)	(0.065)***		
Shea partial *R*-squared	0.55	0.55	0.55		
AP chi-squared test	178.1	178.1	178.1		
p-value	0.000	0.000	0.000		
AP *F*-test	73.1	73.1	58.4		
R-squared	0.82	0.82	0.82		
n	78	78	78		
Hansen *J*-statistic	0.758	0.758	0.757		

SOURCES: Author's estimations using data from Rose (2004); Sala-i-Martin, Doppelhofer, and Miller (2004); Desmet, Ortuño-Ortin, and Wacziarg (2009); Heston, Summers, and Aten (2009); Marshall, Jaggers, and Gurr (2010); World Bank (2010); and OECD, Development Database on Aid from DAC Members: DAC Online (various years).

NOTES: IV-2SLS: IV two-stage least-squares model; IV-LIML: IV limited-information, maximum-likelihood model; IV-Fuller: Fuller's modified LIML model (Baum, Schaffer, and Stillman 2007); AP chi-squared test: the chi-squared test for underidentification of Angrist and Pischke (2009); AP *F*-test: the *F*-test for excluded instruments of Angrist and Pischke (2009). Inter1 means Interaction model 1. This model controls for an interaction of the ratio of aid to GDP with governance (democracy) variable. Inter2 means Interaction model 2. This model controls for interaction of the ratio of aid to GDP with dummies for types of governance regime. Robust standard errors are in parentheses. An empty cell indicates that the corresponding variable is not included in the model. Log means a variable is in logarithmic form. * indicates significant at the 10 percent level; ** indicates significant at the 5 percent level; *** indicates significant at the 1 percent level. All specifications control for East Asian and Sub-Saharan African regional fixed effects. Observations are averages for the 1973–2002 horizon.

TABLE 5.9 Impact of aggregate aid on growth, instrumental variable (IV) tests

	Model 1	Model 2	Model 3	Model 4	Model 5	Model 6
	Panel A: IV estimation (dependent variable: average annual growth)					
Aid/GDP ratio	–0.052	0.047	–0.028	–0.000	–0.018	–0.108
	(0.033)	(0.044)	(0.039)	(0.037)	(0.034)	(0.055)*
Fitted aid/GDP ratio						0.031
						(0.031)
Log initial population		0.313				
		(0.172)*				
Colony of Portugal	0.904					
	(0.626)					
Initial share of agriculture in GDP			0.015			
			(0.016)			
Initial donor exports per capita (log)				–0.193		
				(0.221)		
Initial life expectancy (1960s)					–0.007	
					(0.046)	
F-statistic	11.1	20.3	12.6	14.6	13.2	30.7
R-squared	0.65	0.60	0.64	0.62	0.63	0.64
	Panel B: First-stage regression (dependent variable: total aid/GDP ratio)					
Fitted aid/GDP ratio	0.780	0.677	0.906	0.831	0.840	0.677
	(0.085)***	(0.106)***	(0.077)***	(0.077)***	(0.065)	(0.106)***
Log initial population		–0.982				–0.982
		(0.438)**				(0.438)**

Log area						
Colony of Portugal	2.691 (1.683)					
Initial share of agriculture in GDP			–0.110 (0.033)***			
Initial donor exports per capita (log)				0.129 (0.649)		
Initial life expectancy (1960s)					0.002 (0.138)	
Shea partial *R*-squared	0.49	0.35	0.52	0.50	0.46	0.09
AP chi-squared test	123.2	46.7	160.3	108.1	177.6	
p-value	0.000	0.000	0.000	0.000	0.000	
AP *F*-test	47.4	18.9	64.7	43.6	71.7	
R-squared	0.83	0.84	0.84	0.82	0.82	0.84
n	78	78	78	78	78	78
Hansen *J*-statistic	0.583	0.835	0.848	0.862	0.750	

SOURCES: Author's estimations using data from OECD Rose (2004); Sala-i-Martin, Doppelhofer, and Miller (2004); Desmet, Ortuño-Ortin, and Wacziarg (2009); Heston, Summers, and Aten (2009); Marshall, Jaggers, and Gurr (2010); World Bank (2010); and OECD, Development Database on Aid from DAC Members: DAC Online (various years).

NOTES: AP chi-squared test: the chi-squared test for underidentification of Angrist and Pischke (2009); AP *F*-test: the *F*-test for excluded instruments of Angrist and Pischke (2009). Robust standard errors are in parentheses. An empty cell indicates that the corresponding variable is not included in the model. Log means a variable is in logarithmic form. * indicates significant at the 10 percent level; ** indicates significant at the 5 percent level; *** indicates significant at the 1 percent level. All specifications control for East Asian and Sub-Saharan African regional fixed effects. Other covariates are omitted for presentational simplicity. Observations are averages for the 1973–2002 horizon.

To test whether the colony of Portugal variable passes the exclusion restriction, as suggested by Rajan and Subramanian (2008), I simply include this variable directly in the second-stage regression (Model 1, Table 5.9). This does not alter the magnitude of the estimated coefficient for the ratio of aggregate aid to GDP, and there is no evidence that the colony of Portugal variable is significant at either the first or the second stage. The result of this test suggests that the colony of Portugal variable is not responsible for the results and passes the exclusion restriction.

Given the use of recipients' population size as a scaling variable for measuring influence in the constructed instrument for aid, the next check is to see whether population size passes the exclusion restriction. As mentioned earlier, the component of the constructed aid ratio that is correlated with recipients' population size cannot be used to estimate aid's impact on growth. This is very important because the validity of the constructed instrument in Rajan and Subramanian (2008) was questioned because of this variable. The results provided in Panel A of Table 5.6 and the relevant discussion earlier suggested that the constructed instrument for aggregate aid provided enough information beyond that included in recipients' population size. However, the only way to accurately assess whether the constructed instrument includes information beyond population size is to test whether it retains significance when population size itself is directly included in the growth regression (Frankel and Romer 1999; Bazzi and Clemens 2009). Model 2 (Table 5.9) reruns the growth equation, this time directly, including log initial population in the regression as an explanatory variable. The AP chi-squared and AP *F*-statistics (Panel B) suggest that the instrument still remains very strong when log initial population is directly included in the second-stage regression.

Models 3, 4, and 5 (Table 5.9), respectively, check whether the initial share of agriculture in GDP, initial donor exports, and initial life expectancy pass the exclusion restrictions. Yet again, the AP chi-squared and AP *F*-statistics (Panel B) firmly suggest that the instrument remains very strong when these variables are included in growth regression. The Hansen *J*-statistic suggests that in all these specifications the overidentification restrictions are firmly rejected. Finally, Model 6 (Table 5.9) presents an intuitive way of illustrating the exclusion restriction (as in Acemoglu, Johnson, and Robinson 2001 and Rajan and Subramanian 2008). The first-stage regression is estimated using log initial population as an instrument for aid, and the second-stage regression is estimated directly, including the constructed instrument as an additional explanatory variable. The constructed instrument is insignificant, suggesting that it has no independent effect on growth. Overall, the results of exclusion restriction and overidentification tests show that the constructed instrument is valid. In addition, the coefficient for the aid variable is insignificant in all cases, establishing the robustness of the results.

Disaggregated Aid: Growth Equation

The results of cross-sectional growth regressions, in which aid to economic infrastructure is instrumented with its constructed analog, are presented in Table 5.10. The equations are well specified, and the instrumentation is strong for both aid to economic infrastructure and democracy, as indicated by the Shea partial R-squared, AP chi-squared, and AP F-statistics in Panels B and C of the table. The IV coefficient for the ratio of aid to economic infrastructure to GDP is positive in every specification but statistically insignificant, suggesting that there is no evidence that aid to economic infrastructure directly affects economic growth. Similarly, the estimated parameters on democracy are positive but statistically insignificant at conventional significance levels. The results also suggest that there is no statistically significant interaction effect between democracy and aid to economic infrastructure. Likewise, the estimated coefficients for the interactions of aid to economic infrastructure with different levels of democracy are statistically insignificant, suggesting that the estimated parameters of interest are not different from zero. Therefore, one cannot draw any positive conclusion regarding the effect of aid on economic infrastructure on per capita GDP growth. These findings are consistent with empirical evidence that in developing countries economic growth is primarily input driven and that total factor productivity increases are negligible (Krugman 1994; Young 1995; Collins and Bosworth 1996).

The estimated coefficients for secondary school enrollment are positive and robust across all estimated specifications. The size of the coefficient suggests that an increase of 1 percentage point in secondary school enrollment is associated with a 0.04 percent higher average annual growth rate. On the contrary, the coefficients for investment ratio are all positive but statistically insignificant. However, from these results we cannot make any causal interpretations because of endogeneity between these variables and economic growth. Among other results, average initial inflation and revolutions are negatively related to economic growth.

Table 5.11 shows the results of the tests for exclusion restrictions. These tests are performed much as in the aggregate aid case. The first thing to note is that the colony of Portugal variable (Model 1), population size (Model 2), initial share of agriculture in GDP (Model 3), and initial donor exports (Model 4) readily pass the exclusion restriction tests. Second, Hansen's J-statistic fails to reject overidentification restrictions at the conventional significance levels, suggesting that the instrument is valid and the equation is not overidentified. Third, the constructed instrument has no independent effect on economic growth (Model 5). Finally, the coefficient for aid to economic infrastructure is insignificant in the estimated specifications, confirming the robustness of the core results.

TABLE 5.10 Impact of disaggregated aid on growth, instrumental variable (IV) estimations

	IV-2SLS	IV-LIML	IV-Fuller	Inter1	Inter2
Panel A: IV estimation (dependent variable: average annual growth of per capita GDP)					
Infrastructure aid/GDP ratio	0.638	0.652	0.618	0.352	0.346
	(0.436)	(0.445)	(0.422)	(0.363)	(0.484)
Governance	0.183	0.185	0.181	0.390	0.154
	(0.305)	(0.310)	(0.298)	(0.542)	(0.380)
Infrastructure aid/GDP ratio × governance				–0.236	
				(0.288)	
Infrastructure aid/GDP ratio × partially free					–0.056
					(0.430)
Infrastructure aid/GDP ratio × not free					0.106
					(0.433)
Initial GDP per capita (log)	–0.533	–0.518	–0.556	–0.884	–0.891
	(0.723)	(0.732)	(0.711)	(0.543)	(0.525)*
Initial life expectancy (1960s)	0.026	0.026	0.026	0.017	0.021
	(0.028)	(0.028)	(0.028)	(0.027)	(0.027)
School enrollment	0.043	0.043	0.043	0.043	0.042
	(0.012)***	(0.012)***	(0.012)***	(0.013)***	(0.012)***
Openness	–2.885	–2.917	–2.837	–1.776	–1.893
	(1.562)*	(1.579)*	(1.539)*	(1.390)	(1.254)
Investment ratio	0.033	0.033	0.034	0.033	0.034
	(0.024)	(0.025)	(0.025)	(0.027)	(0.029)
Average inflation	–0.039	–0.039	–0.038	–0.032	–0.027
	(0.013)**	(0.013)**	(0.013)**	(0.014)**	(0.011)**
Geography (absolute latitude)	–0.006	–0.006	–0.005	0.001	0.004
	(0.020)	(0.021)	(0.020)	(0.020)	(0.022)
Coastal population density in 1965	0.002	0.002	0.002	0.001	0.001
	(0.001)**	(0.001)**	(0.001)**	(0.001)	(0.001)
Malaria risk in 1966	–0.218	–0.216	–0.222	–0.270	–0.202
	(0.568)	(0.569)	(0.566)	(0.570)	(0.623)
Revolutions	–1.992	–1.996	–1.996	–1.852	–1.831
	(0.860)**	(0.864)**	(0.864)**	(0.850)**	(0.795)**
Constant	2.084	1.960	2.265	4.015	4.695
Test for interactions (*p*-value)				0.515	0.665

F-statistic (overall model)	12.8	12.8	12.9	13.9	12.7
R-squared	0.60	0.59	0.60	0.59	0.58
Panel B: First-stage regression (dependent variable: infrastructure aid/GDP ratio)					
Fitted infrastructure aid/GDP ratio	0.532	0.532	0.532	***	***
	(0.071)***	(0.071)***	(0.071)***		
Shea partial R-squared	0.40	0.40	0.40		
AP chi-squared test	69.0	69.0	69.0		
p-value	0.000	0.000	0.000		
AP F-test	40.8	40.8	40.8		
R-squared	0.84	0.84	0.84		
Panel C: First-stage regression (dependent variable: democracy score)					
Initial level of executive constraint	0.277	0.277	0.277	***	***
	(0.054)***	(0.054)***	(0.054)***		
Indicator for countries that gained independence after 1945	–0.914	–0.914	–0.914		
	(0.283)***	(0.283)***	(0.283)***		
Shea partial R-squared	0.36	0.36	0.36		
AP chi-squared (underidentification test)	40.8	40.8	40.8		
p-value	0.000	0.000	0.000		
AP F-test of excluded instruments	16.0	16.0	16.0		
R-squared	0.65	0.65	0.65		
n	72	72	72	72	72
Hansen J-statistic (p-value)	0.528	0.528	0.528		

SOURCES: Author's estimations using data from Rose (2004); Sala-i-Martin, Doppelhofer, and Miller (2004); Desmet, Ortuño-Ortin, and Wacziarg (2009); Heston, Summers, and Aten (2009); Marshall, Jaggers, and Gurr (2010); World Bank (2010); and OECD, Development Database on Aid Activities: CRS Online (various years).

NOTES: IV-2SLS: IV two-stage least-squares model; IV-LIML: IV limited-information, maximum-likelihood model; IV-Fuller: Fuller's modified LIML model (Baum, Schaffer, and Stillman 2007); AP chi-squared test: the chi-squared test for underidentification of Angrist and Pischke (2009); AP F-test: the F-test for excluded instruments of Angrist and Pischke (2009). Inter1 means Interaction model 1. This model controls for an interaction of the ratio of aid to GDP with governance (democracy) variable. Inter2 means Interaction model 2. This model controls for interaction of the ratio of aid to GDP with dummies for types of governance regime. Robust standard errors are in parentheses. An empty cell indicates that the corresponding variable is not included in the model. Log means a variable is in logarithmic form. * indicates significant at the 10 percent level; ** indicates significant at the 5 percent level; *** indicates significant at the 1 percent level. All specifications control for East Asian and Sub-Saharan African regional fixed effects. Other covariates are omitted for presentational simplicity. Observations are averages for the 1973–2002 horizon.

TABLE 5.11 Impact of disaggregated aid on growth, instrumental variable (IV) tests

	Model 1	Model 2	Model 3	Model 4	Model 5
Panel A: IV estimation (dependent variable: average annual growth rate of per capita GDP)					
Infrastructure aid/GDP ratio	0.595 (0.591)	1.118 (0.591)*	0.312 (0.286)	0.669 (0.440)	–1.278 (0.987)
Fitted infrastructure aid/GDP ratio					1.003 (0.642)
Log initial population		0.500 (0.266)*			
Colony of Portugal	0.214 (1.103)				
Initial share of agriculture in GDP			0.024 (0.024)		
Initial donor exports per capita (log)				–0.078 (0.230)	
F-statistic	11.8	9.9	16.7	11.9	16.2
R-squared	0.60	0.56	0.66	0.59	0.66
Panel B: First-stage regression (dependent variable: economic aid/GDP ratio)					
Fitted infrastructure aid/GDP ratio	0.431 (0.084)***	0.419 (0.102)***	0.543 (0.068)***	0.548 (0.077)***	

Log initial population		–0.209			–0.311
		(0.082)**			(0.065)***
Colony of Portugal	0.709				
	(0.241)**				
Initial share of agriculture in GDP			–0.003		
			(0.008)		
Initial donor exports per capita (log)				–0.140	
				(0.101)	
Shea partial *R*-squared	0.24	0.26	0.43	0.43	
AP chi-squared test	34.0	21.4	89.0	61.8	
p-value	0.000	0.000	0.000	0.000	
AP *F*-test	13.1	16.8	33.2	23.8	
R-squared	0.85	0.86	0.86	0.85	0.86
n	72	72	67	72	72
Hansen *J*-statistic	0.529	0.601	0.534	0.545	

SOURCES: Author's estimations using data from Rose (2004); Sala-i-Martin, Doppelhofer, and Miller (2004); Desmet, Ortuño-Ortin, and Wacziarg (2009); Heston, Summers, and Aten (2009); Marshall, Jaggers, and Gurr (2010); World Bank (2010); and OECD, Development Database on Aid Activities: CRS Online (various years).

NOTES: AP chi-squared test: the chi-squared test for underidentification of Angrist and Pischke (2009); AP *F*-test: the *F*-test for excluded instruments of Angrist and Pischke (2009). Robust standard errors are in parentheses. An empty cell indicates that the corresponding variable is not included in the model. Log means a variable is in logarithmic form. * indicates significant at the 10 percent level; ** indicates significant at the 5 percent level; *** indicates significant at the 1 percent level. All specifications control for East Asian and Sub-Saharan African regional fixed effects. Other covariates are omitted for presentational simplicity. Observations are averages for the 1973–2002 horizon.

Investment Equation

Table 5.12 provides the results of IV regressions for the investment equation. The first-stage results suggest that the equation is well specified and that instrumentation for economic aid, as well as for democracy, is strong as indicated by the Shea partial *R*-squared, AP chi-squared, and AP *F*-statistics in Panels B (for economic aid) and C (for democracy) of Table 5.12. The first-stage AP chi-squared test promptly rejects its null hypothesis, and the AP *F*-statistics are well above the rule-of-thumb threshold of 10 proposed by Staiger and Stock (1997). Naturally, the LIML and Fuller's modified LIML estimates are very similar to the 2SLS regression results. Similar to the OLS results (Table 5.3), the IV estimates suggest that the impact of economic aid on the ratio of investment to GDP is positive and statistically significant. However, the magnitude of the coefficient is considerably higher than the OLS results. The 2SLS estimate suggests that in the long run an increase of 1 percentage point in the ratio of economic aid to GDP leads to a 2.3 percentage point higher ratio of investment to GDP.

The estimated coefficients for democracy and its interactions with economic aid are positive but statistically insignificant at conventional significance levels. Similarly, the interactions of economic aid with different levels of democracy are statistically insignificant. These results are also quite different from the OLS regression results, which suggested that economic aid is more beneficial for investment in partially free and not free countries. The remaining results suggest that countries with higher initial per capita income, higher initial financial depth, and higher ratios of FDI to GDP are more likely to invest more. On the other hand, political instability and revolutions seem to have a negative effect on the ratio of investment to GDP. The estimated coefficients for the initial level of trade policy (Sachs-Warner) are statistically insignificant.

Table 5.13 provides a summary of the exclusion restriction tests for the investment equation. First, adding the colony of Portugal variable directly in the regression equation (Model 1) changes the estimated coefficient for the ratio of economic aid to GDP upward but does not affect its sign, and there is no evidence that this colonial variable is significant at the second stage. Second, to accurately test whether the constructed instrument retains its significance when the population size variable is directly included in the first-stage regression, Model 2 (Table 5.13) reruns the investment equation, this time directly including the logarithm of initial population in the first-stage regression. The AP chi-squared statistic successfully rejects its null hypothesis, suggesting that the equation is not underidentified. The first-stage AP *F*-statistic suggests that the constructed instrument's strength declines when log initial population is included in the equation but still retains its relevance. However, the first-stage AP *F*-statistic is only 6.9, which is below the threshold of 10. On the plus side, the 2SLS estimate and standard error are fairly similar to the LIML estimate and standard error (not reported). Moreover, the estimated coefficient for the ratio of economic aid to GDP is fairly similar to the original estimates in Table 5.12 (without including log initial population), and there is no evidence that population size is significant at the second stage. This allows us to conclude that the constructed instrument remains practically relevant even after including the population size in the regression equation.[8]

Further, Models 3 and 4 show the results of exclusion restriction tests for the initial share of agriculture and initial donor exports. Both variables easily pass the exclusion restriction test based on the first-stage AP chi-squared and AP F-statistics. The inclusion of these variables in the regression equation does not seriously alter the magnitude of the estimated coefficient for the ratio of economic aid to GDP. Overall, the results of the previously mentioned tests show that the constructed instrument for economic aid is valid, and it firmly holds its strength when suspect variables are included in the regression equation. It is also worth noting that Hansen's J-statistic shows that the instrument also readily satisfies the overidentification restrictions. Moreover, the coefficient for the ratio of economic aid to GDP is positive and significant in all specifications, establishing the robustness of the results. Additionally, the sign of the democracy variable does not change and is still insignificant (not reported).

Finally, Model 5 presents an intuitive way of testing whether the constructed instrument has an independent impact on domestic investment. The first-stage regression is estimated using log initial population as an excluded instrument for the ratio of economic aid to GDP, and the second-stage investment regression is estimated directly, including the constructed instrument as an additional explanatory variable. The constructed instrument is insignificant, suggesting that it has no independent effect on the ratio of investment to GDP.

Schooling Equation

The IV estimates of cross-sectional schooling regressions are provided in Table 5.14. The results in the first two columns are obtained using the 2SLS and the LIML estimators, respectively. In these regressions the social aid is instrumented with the ratio of constructed social aid to GDP and governance is instrumented with the level of constraints on the executive in 1900 and an indicator for countries that gained independence after 1945. The overidentification restrictions are not rejected at conventional levels of significance, as suggested by Hansen's J-statistic. The first-stage results suggest that instrumentation for social aid is strong, as indicated by the AP chi-squared and AP F-statistics shown in Panel B of Table 5.14. However, the first-stage AP F-statistics (Panel C) suggest that the instruments for the democracy variable could be weak. The

8. Angrist and Pischke (2009) suggest that one cannot always rely on a mechanical rule, such as $F > 10$, to determine instrument relevance. In some cases, an F statistic below 10 may not be a problem.

TABLE 5.12 Impact of economic aid on investment, instrumental variable (IV) estimations

	IV-2SLS	IV-LIML	IV-Fuller	Inter 1	Inter 2
Panel A: IV Estimation, second stage (dependent variable: average annual investment/GDP ratio)					
Economic aid/GDP ratio	2.313	2.343	2.309	2.471	2.533
	(0.603)***	(0.624)***	(0.600)***	(0.773)***	(0.626)***
Governance	2.286	2.337	2.280	1.763	2.186
	(1.531)	(1.569)	(1.526)	(1.498)	(1.609)
Economic aid/GDP ratio × governance				0.086	
				(0.523)	
Economic aid/GDP ratio × free					–0.829
					(0.901)
Economic aid/GDP ratio × partially free					0.289
					(0.552)
Initial GDP per capita (log)	3.708	3.729	3.705	4.352	4.193
	(1.880)**	(1.924)**	(1.874)**	(2.083)**	(2.060)**
Initial level of policy (Sachs-Warner)	–2.087	–2.152	–2.079	–1.465	–1.423
	(3.232)	(3.253)	(3.230)	(3.149)	(3.267)
Initial financial depth	0.199	0.200	0.199	0.189	0.193
	(0.082)**	(0.082)**	(0.082)**	(0.087)**	(0.093)**
Average inflation (1960–90)	–0.042	–0.042	–0.042	–0.045	–0.051
	(0.034)	(0.034)	(0.034)	(0.036)	(0.036)
FDI/GDP ratio	0.830	0.825	0.831	0.825	0.756
	(0.353)**	(0.352)**	(0.353)**	(0.408)**	(0.392)*
Revolutions	–5.930	–5.902	–5.934	–5.994	–5.664
	(3.388)*	(3.418)*	(3.385)*	(2.741)**	(2.782)
Constant	–26.011	–26.453	–25.956	–28.830	–29.456
Test for interactions (*p*-value)				0.000	0.000
F-statistic (overall model)	23.0	22.9	23.0	25.4	19.9
R-squared	0.64	0.64	0.64	0.69	0.69

Panel B: First-stage regression (dependent variable: economic aid/GDP ratio)					
Fitted economic aid/GDP ratio	0.573	0.573	0.573	***	***
	(0.094)***	(0.094)***	(0.094)***		
Shea partial *R*-squared	0.32	0.32	0.32		
AP chi-squared test	43.7	43.7	43.7		
p-value	0.000	0.000	0.000		
AP *F*-test	18.6	18.6	18.6		
R-squared	0.74	0.74	0.74		
Panel C: First-stage regression (dependent variable: democracy score)					
Initial level of executive constraint	0.287	0.287	0.287	***	***
	(0.049)***	(0.049)***	(0.049)***		
Indicator for countries that gained independence after 1945	–0.949	–0.949	–0.949		
	(0.236)***	(0.236)***	(0.236)***		
Shea partial *R*-squared	0.39	0.39	0.39		
AP chi-squared test	52.9	52.9	52.9		
p-value	0.000	0.000	0.000		
AP *F*-test	22.5	22.5	22.5		
R-squared	0.70	0.70	0.7		
n	80	80	80		
Hansen *J*-statistic	0.347	0.347	0.347		

SOURCES: Author's estimations using data from Rose (2004); Sala-i-Martin, Doppelhofer, and Miller (2004); Desmet, Ortuño-Ortin, and Wacziarg (2009); Heston, Summers, and Aten (2009); Marshall, Jaggers, and Gurr (2010); World Bank (2010); and OECD, Development Database on Aid Activities: CRS Online (various years).

NOTES: IV-2SLS: IV two-stage least-squares model; IV-LIML: IV limited-information, maximum-likelihood model; IV-Fuller: Fuller's modified LIML model (Baum, Schaffer, and Stillman 2007); FDI: stands for foreign direct investment; AP chi-squared test: the chi-squared test for underidentification of Angrist and Pischke (2009); AP *F*-test: the *F*-test for excluded instruments of Angrist and Pischke (2009). Inter1 means Interaction model 1. This model controls for an interaction of the ratio of aid to GDP with governance (democracy) variable. Inter2 means Interaction model 2. This model controls for interaction of the ratio of aid to GDP with dummies for types of governance regime. Robust standard errors are in parentheses. An empty cell indicates that the corresponding variable is not included in the model. Log means a variable is in logarithmic form. * indicates significant at the 10 percent level; ** indicates significant at the 5 percent level; *** indicates significant at the 1 percent level. Other covariates are omitted for presentational simplicity. Observations are averages for the 1973–2002 horizon.

TABLE 5.13 Impact of economic aid on investment, instrumental variable (IV) tests

	Model 1	Model 2	Model 3	Model 4	Model 5
Panel A: IV estimation (dependent variable: average annual investment/GDP ratio)					
Economic aid/GDP ratio	3.138	2.590	2.375	2.379	1.220
	(0.909)***	(1.283)**	(0.611)***	(0.645)***	(0.953)
Fitted economic aid/GDP ratio					0.872
					(0.620)
Log initial population		0.471			
		(1.419)			
Colony of Portugal	–7.586				
	(4.356)*				
Initial share of agriculture in GDP			–0.025		
			(0.068)		
Initial donor exports per capita (log)				–0.289	
				(0.908)	
F-statistic	19.6	19.0	17.1	20.6	13.9
R-squared	0.62	0.67	0.68	0.64	0.64
Panel B: First-stage regression (dependent variable: economic aid/GDP ratio)					
Fitted economic aid/GDP ratio	0.630	0.307	0.651	0.568	
	(0.125)***	(0.117)**	(0.093)***	(0.098)***	

Log initial population		–0.613 (0.147)***			–0.811 (0.121)
Colony of Portugal	0.317 (0.818)				
Initial share of agriculture in GDP			–0.030 (0.013)**		
Initial donor exports per capita (log)				0.043 (0.186)	
Shea partial R-squared	0.27	0.10	0.35	0.30	
AP chi-squared test	33.1	8.1	58.6	38.0	
p-value	0.000	0.004	0.000	0.000	
AP F-test	9.2	6.9	24.5	15.9	
R-squared	0.75	0.79	0.75	0.74	0.75
n	80	80	80	80	80
Hansen J-statistic	0.402	0.728	0.337	0.346	

SOURCES: Author's estimations using data from Rose (2004); Sala-i-Martin, Doppelhofer, and Miller (2004); Desmet, Ortuño-Ortin, and Wacziarg (2009); Heston, Summers, and Aten (2009); Marshall, Jaggers, and Gurr (2010); World Bank (2010); and OECD, Development Database on Aid Activities: CRS Online (various years).

NOTES: AP chi-squared test: the chi-squared test for underidentification of Angrist and Pischke (2009); AP F-test: the F-test for excluded instruments of Angrist and Pischke (2009). Robust standard errors are in parentheses. An empty cell indicates that the corresponding variable is not included in the model. Log means a variable is in logarithmic form. * indicates significant at the 10 percent level; ** indicates significant at the 5 percent level; *** indicates significant at the 1 percent level. All specifications control for East Asian and Sub-Saharan African regional fixed effects. Other covariates are omitted for presentational simplicity. Observations are averages for the 1973–2002 horizon.

TABLE 5.14 Impact of social aid on schooling, instrumental variable (IV) estimations

	IV-2SLS	IV-LIML	IV-2SLS*	Inter1	Inter2
Panel A: IV estimation, second stage (dependent variable: secondary school enrollment)					
Social aid/GDP ratio	–0.215	–0.216	–0.157	–0.214	
	(1.256)	(1.258)	(1.240)	(1.335)	
Governance	1.213	1.217	0.815	1.198	–0.472
	(3.750)	(3.760)	(4.047)	(3.952)	(3.964)
Social aid/GDP ratio × governance				0.123	
				(1.062)	
Social aid/GDP ratio × free					2.231
					(1.878)
Social aid/GDP ratio × partially free					–1.025
					(1.606)
Social aid/GDP ratio × not free					–0.773
					(1.601)
Initial secondary enrollment	0.768	0.768	0.767	0.769	0.781
	(0.151)***	(0.151)***	(0.149)***	(0.163)***	(0.162)***
Initial income per capita (log)	7.998	7.998	8.151	7.977	8.415
	(3.082)***	(3.082)***	(3.025)***	(3.372)**	(3.220)***
Infant mortality	6.873	6.873	6.917	6.750	7.300
	(3.285)**	(3.285)**	(3.261)**	(3.837)*	(3.541)**
Average fertility	–7.930	–7.927	–8.206	–7.962	8.603
	(3.400)**	(3.405)**	(3.503)**	(3.595)**	(3.677)**
Malaria risk in 1966	–11.521	–11.524	–11.258	–11.522	–12.758
	(4.942)**	(4.947)**	(5.211)**	(5.453)**	(5.385)**
Education expenditures (percent of GDP)	–0.826	–0.826	–0.813	–0.850	–1.072
	(1.099)	(1.100)	(1.066)	(1.148)	(1.267)
Population under 15 (percent)	0.753	0.753	0.771	0.756	0.840
	(0.454)*	(0.454)*	(0.444)*	(0.500)	(0.510)
Constant	–50.651	–50.653	–50.074	–49.843	–48.666
Test for interactions (*p*-value)				0.992	0.657
F-statistic (overall model)	59.7	59.7	61.4	57.1	49.8
R-squared	0.86	0.86	0.86	0.86	0.87

Panel B: First-stage regression (dependent variable: social aid/GDP ratio)					
Fitted social aid/GDP ratio	1.231	1.231	1.222	***	***
	(0.235)***	(0.235)***	(0.231)***		
Shea partial R-squared	0.37	0.37	0.35		
AP chi-squared test	24.5	24.5	22.6		
p-value	0.000	0.000	0.000		
AP F-test	10.2	10.2	19.0		
R-squared	0.77	0.77	0.76		
Panel C: First-stage regression (dependent variable: democracy score)					
Initial level of executive constraint	0.186	0.186	0.144	***	***
	(0.054)***	(0.054)***	(0.049)***		
Indicator for countries that gained independence after 1945	–0.622	–0.622			
	(0.311)**	(0.311)**			
Shea partial R-squared	0.13	0.13	0.09		
AP chi-squared test	13.0	13.0	9.2		
p-value	0.001	0.001	0.002		
AP F-test	5.4	5.4	7.7		
R-squared	0.55	0.55	0.52		
n	76	76	76		
Hansen J-statistic	0.877	0.877	***		

SOURCES: Author's estimations using data from Rose (2004); Sala-i-Martin, Doppelhofer, and Miller (2004); Desmet, Ortuño-Ortin, and Wacziarg (2009); Heston, Summers, and Aten (2009); Marshall, Jaggers, and Gurr (2010); World Bank (2010); and OECD, Development Database on Aid Activities: CRS Online (various years).

NOTES: IV-2SLS: IV two-stage least-squares model, in which governance (democracy) is instrumented with the level of constraints on the executive in 1900 and is an indicator for countries that gained independence after 1945; IV-2SLS*: IV two-stage least-squares model, in which governance (democracy) is instrumented with the level of constraints on the executive in 1900 only; IV-LIML: IV limited-information, maximum-likelihood model; IV-Fuller: Fuller's modified LIML model (Baum, Schaffer, and Stillman 2007); AP chi-squared test: the chi-squared test for underidentification of Angrist and Pischke (2009); AP F-test indicates the F-test for excluded instruments of Angrist and Pischke (2009). Inter1 means Interaction model 1. This model controls for an interaction of the ratio of aid to GDP with governance (democracy) variable. Inter2 means Interaction model 2. This model controls for interaction of the ratio of aid to GDP with dummies for types of governance regime. Robust standard errors are in parentheses. An empty cell indicates that the corresponding variable is not included in the model. Log means a variable is in logarithmic form. * indicates significant at the 10 percent level; ** indicates significant at the 5 percent level; *** indicates significant at the 1 percent level. All specifications control for East Asian and Sub-Saharan African regional fixed effects. Other covariates are omitted for presentational simplicity. Observations are averages for the 1973–2002 horizon.

first stage's coefficients for individual democracy instruments and other covariates suggest that this weakness could be related to the indicator for countries that gained independence after 1945. That is why I re-estimated the equation by removing this indicator from the equation and instrumenting the democracy variable only with the level of constraints on the executive in 1900. The results that are obtained from this model are reported in the third column (IV-2SLS*). As can be seen in Table 5.14, the results of the 2SLS estimator are nearly identical to the LIML estimates. The results remain qualitatively unchanged when a slightly different instrumentation strategy with respect to the governance variable is implemented. Moreover, the standard errors in these three alternative estimates are not much different from each other.

The estimated coefficients for the ratio of social aid to GDP are statistically insignificant in all specifications. Similarly, the estimated coefficients for democracy and its interactions with the ratio of social aid to GDP are statistically insignificant at conventional significance levels. These results remain qualitatively similar when secondary school enrollment is replaced with primary school enrollment or average years of schooling as a dependent variable. The other results are also qualitatively similar to the OLS estimates. For example, the estimates suggest that there is significant inertia in secondary school enrollment. Not surprisingly, initial per capita income has the expected positive impact on school enrollment. Average fertility has a negative association with school enrollment, intuitively suggesting that a higher average fertility rate would put pressure on the education system and would thus be expected to reduce enrollment rates. In addition, a higher average fertility rate would require more public expenditures (from both domestic and foreign sources) on reproduction and healthcare systems, reducing the pool of public resources available for education.

Table 5.15 reports the results of exclusion restriction tests. These tests are performed similarly to those discussed previously. All four suspect variables, including population size (Model 1), initial ratio of physicians to the population (Model 2), initial average level of access to water (Model 3), and initial fertility (Model 4), passed the exclusion restriction tests. Further, the intuitive test suggests that the constructed instrument for the ratio of social aid to GDP has no independent effect on secondary school enrollment (Model 5). Finally, the coefficient for social aid is insignificant in all four cases, further confirming the robustness of the core results.

System of Simultaneous Equations Results

The IV results provided earlier are obtained assuming that there is no correlation between the error terms for the growth, investment, and human capital equations. However, as mentioned earlier, apart from issues of endogeneity among aid, governance, and growth, some variables are jointly determined in

TABLE 5.15 Impact of social aid on schooling, independent variable (IV) tests

	Model 1	Model 2	Model 3	Model 4	Model 5
Panel A: IV estimation, second stage (dependent variable: secondary school enrollment)					
Social aid/GDP ratio	0.597 (2.461)	–0.273 (1.284)	–0.163 (1.197)	–2.195 (1.728)	–0.943 (3.026)
Fitted social aid/GDP ratio					0.932 (2.641)
Log initial population	0.841 (2.022)				
Initial ratio of physicians to population		–1.342 (4.563)			
Initial access to water			0.203 (0.107)*		
Initial fertility				2.859 (4.047)	
F-statistic	55.1	56.2	55.8	44.9	58.0
R-squared	0.86	0.86	0.87	0.80	0.86
Panel B: First-stage regression (dependent variable: social aid/GDP ratio)					
Fitted social aid/GDP ratio	1.081 (0.269)***	1.260 (0.243)***	1.232 (0.229)***	1.186 (0.216)***	

(continued)

TABLE 5.15 Continued

	Model 1	Model 2	Model 3	Model 4	Model 5
Log initial population	–0.131				–0.663
	(0.126)				(0.160)***
Initial ratio of physicians to population		0.787			
		(0.501)			
Initial access to water			0.012		
			(0.010)		
Initial fertility				–0.273	
				(0.204)	
Shea partial *R*-squared	0.25	0.37	0.38	0.41	
AP chi-squared test	17.3	23.8	26.9	32.4	
p-value	0.000	0.000	0.000	0.000	
AP *F*-test of	7.1	9.7	11.0	13.4	
R-squared	0.77	0.77	0.77	0.76	0.69
n	76	76	76	76	76
Hansen *J*-statistic	0.957	0.781	0.594	0.843	

SOURCES: Author's estimations using data from Rose (2004); Sala-i-Martin, Doppelhofer, and Miller (2004); Desmet, Ortuño-Ortin, and Wacziarg (2009); Heston, Summers, and Aten (2009); Marshall, Jaggers, and Gurr (2010); World Bank (2010); and OECD, Development Database on Aid Activities: CRS Online (various years).

NOTES: AP chi-squared test: the chi-squared test for underidentification of Angrist and Pischke (2009); AP *F*-test: the *F*-test for excluded instruments of Angrist and Pischke (2009). Robust standard errors are in parentheses. An empty cell indicates that the corresponding variable is not included in the model. Log means a variable is in logarithmic form. * indicates significant at the 10 percent level; ** indicates significant at the 5 percent level; *** indicates significant at the 1 percent level. All specifications control for East Asian and Sub-Saharan African regional fixed effects. Other covariates are omitted for presentational simplicity. Observations are averages for the 1973–2002 horizon.

these equations. The ratios of investment to GDP and secondary school enrollment are dependent variables in the investment and schooling equations, respectively. At the same time, they appear as explanatory variables in the growth equation. This creates endogeneity between these variables and economic growth. Moreover, some right-hand-side variables are included in all three equations. As a result, the error terms of these three equations will be correlated. Moreover, the endogenous variables could be correlated with the disturbance term. Therefore, the single-equation IV estimate discussed earlier could still be biased and inconsistent.

To cope with these issues, in this section I implement a simultaneous equations approach that allows me to simultaneously solve the growth, investment, and schooling equations using the 3SLS estimator. In this system of structural equations framework, instrumentation for aid components is done at the first stage, the investment and schooling equations are estimated at the second (intermediate) stage, and the growth equation is estimated at the third stage. The predicted values of the investment ratio and secondary school enrollment are used to replace the investment ratio and (contemporaneous) school enrollment in the per capita GDP growth equation. Overall, this simultaneous equations system includes six equations: the first three equations for instrumentation of aid to economic infrastructure, economic aid, and social aid, respectively, and the remaining three equations for growth, investment, and schooling, respectively. The results of these estimates are reported in Table 5.16. The results of the standard OLS and the single-equation IV regressions are also provided for comparison.

TABLE 5.16 System of simultaneous equations estimates

	OLS	SE-IV	SSE-IV
	Panel A: Growth equation		
Infrastructure aid/GDP ratio	–0.294	0.632	–0.005
	(0.267)	(0.436)	(0.345)
Investment	0.056	0.033	0.123
	(0.024)**	(0.024)	(0.042)**
School enrollment	0.023	0.043	0.047
	(0.009)**	(0.012)***	(0.016)***
Governance	0.226	0.183	0.480
	(0.221)	(0.305)	(0.268)*
Initial GDP per capita (log)	–1.510	–0.533	–2.030
	(0.419)***	(0.723)	(0.580)***
n	73	72	68
F-statistic	9.2	12.8	9.3
R-squared	0.58	0.60	0.58

(*continued*)

TABLE 5.16 Continued

	OLS	SE-IV	SSE-IV
Panel B: Investment equation			
Economic aid/GDP ratio	1.595	2.313	2.170
	(0.595)**	(0.603)***	(0.548)***
Governance	0.553	2.286	0.835
	(0.833)	(1.531)	(1.155)
Initial GDP per capita (log)	3.765	3.708	6.301
	(1.114)**	(1.880)**	(1.740)***
n	81	80	68
F-statistic	21.1	23.0	14.9
R-squared	0.68	0.64	0.65
Panel C: Schooling (secondary school enrollment) equation			
Social aid/GDP ratio	–0.121	–0.215	0.358
	(0.748)	(1.256)	(1.082)
Governance	–0.311	1.213	–0.126
	(1.880)	(3.750)	(2.242)
Initial GDP per capita (log)	8.456	7.998	6.680
	(2.556)***	(3.082)***	(3.138)**
Initial secondary schooling (1970s)	0.764	0.768	0.828
	(0.159)***	(0.151)***	(0.130)***
n	76	76	68
F-statistic	56.7	59.7	38.7
R-squared	0.86	0.86	0.86

SOURCES: Author's estimations using data from Rose (2004); Sala-i-Martin, Doppelhofer, and Miller (2004); Desmet, Ortuño-Ortin, and Wacziarg (2009); Heston, Summers, and Aten (2009); Marshall, Jaggers, and Gurr (2010); World Bank (2010); and OECD, Development Database on Aid Activities: CRS Online (various years).

NOTES: The simultaneous system of equations instrumental variable (SSE-IV) estimates are obtained in Stata using the reg3 command with three-stage least-squares (3SLS) option. Single-equation IV (SE-IV) estimates are from Table 5.10 (Model 1), Table 5.12 (Model 1), and Table 5.14 (Model 1), respectively. Standard ordinary least-squares (OLS) estimates are from Table 5.2 (Model 1), Table 5.3 (Model 1), and Table 5.4 (Model 1), respectively. All specifications control for other covariates and for East Asian and Sub-Saharan African regional fixed effects. Other covariates are omitted for presentation simplicity. Robust standard errors are in parentheses. Observations are averages for the 1973–2002 horizon. Log means a variable is in logarithmic form. * indicates significant at the 10 percent level; ** indicates significant at the 5 percent level; *** indicates significant at the 1 percent level.

Overall, the results of the 3SLS estimator, in the simultaneous system of equations IV (SSE-IV) column, are qualitatively somewhat similar to those in the single-equation IV (SE-IV) column and the OLS column. Not surprisingly, however, the magnitudes of the individual coefficients are different. This suggests that the correlations between the error terms and the endogenous variables, as well as the correlations between the error terms among equations, were creating a bias in the SE-IV estimations. The 3SLS estimates of the parameters of the growth equation confirm that the direct impact of aid to economic infrastructure on per capita GDP growth is insignificant.

The 3SLS regression results indicate that the ratio of investment to GDP has a positive causal effect on the long-term average growth rates of per capita GDP. The estimated coefficient suggests that an increase of 1 percentage point in the ratio of investment to GDP leads to a 0.12 percent increase in the long-run per capita growth rate. In turn, the 3SLS regression results for the investment equation reinforce the results of the SE-IV regression concerning the impact of economic aid on the ratio of investment to GDP. The 3SLS estimate of this coefficient is considerably higher than the standard OLS estimate (column 1) and hence a bit closer to the SE-IV estimate (column 2). The estimated coefficient suggests that an increase of 1 percentage point in the ratio of economic aid to GDP is associated with a 2.17 percentage point increase in the ratio of investment to GDP. Combining these two results, it is possible to say that an increase of 1 percentage point in the ratio of economic aid to GDP increases the long-run per capita growth rate by 0.27 (2.17×0.123) percent. This is very close to a theoretical upper limit for the impact of aggregate aid on growth calculated by Rajan and Subramanian (2008). In their theoretical investigations, they assumed that all aid is invested.[9] However, this assumption is not plausible for aggregate aid because considerable shares of aid are intended for consumption (for example, food aid), technical assistance, and other similar purposes. It is more plausible to assume that all or most of the economic aid is invested.

Further, the 3SLS results suggest that an increase of 1 percentage point in secondary school enrollment causes a 0.05 percent increase in the long-run per capita growth rate. However, one cannot link this positive effect with aid to the social sector based on the 3SLS regression results reported in Panel C of Table 5.16. The results for the schooling equation suggest that there is no statistically positive relationship between the ratio of social aid to GDP and secondary school enrollment. The key findings of the analysis in this section suggest that one should take the endogeneity of key variables seriously. The correlations between the error terms and the endogenous variables, as well as the correlation between the error terms among equations, may considerably alter the results.

---

9. For details, see Appendix C in Rajan and Subramanian (2008, 664).

Panel Results

This section reports the results of the dynamic panel difference GMM and the system GMM regression results.[10] These estimators assume that the initial conditions remain informative and appropriate in the presence of endogenous regressors. The validity of the estimated models was tested by applying Hansen's *J*-statistic, difference-in-Hansen tests, and the Arellano-Bond test of second-order autocorrelation.

Growth Equation

Tables 5.17 and 5.18 present the results of the difference GMM and the system GMM estimations of the growth equation, respectively. These panel regression results correspond to the cross-section results in Table 5.10. In these regressions aid, governance, the investment ratio, school enrollment, infant mortality, inflation, and openness are treated as endogenous and instrumented with GMM-style instruments. Constraints on the executive in 1900, having gained independence after 1945, geography, and ethnic fractionalization are used as strictly exogenous instruments. In order to keep the number of instruments smaller than the number of groups, in the system GMM regressions the GMM-style instruments are collapsed.

In both the difference GMM and the system GMM regressions, the estimated coefficient for the ratio of aid to economic infrastructure to GDP is statistically insignificant at conventional significance levels, confirming the results of the cross-section regressions. Likewise, the results of the dynamic panel interaction models are very similar to the cross-section results. The coefficients for interactions of aid to economic infrastructure with three governance categories (free, partially free, and autocracy) also suggest similar conclusions. The various estimates from both procedures suggest that there is a statistically significant positive link between the ratio of investment to GDP and per capita GDP growth, which again confirms the cross-section regression results. However, the magnitude of the estimated coefficients, especially the system GMM results, is slightly higher than the cross-section estimate. In fact, both the system GMM and the difference GMM results with respect to the impact of secondary school enrollment on per capita growth are statistically insignificant at conventional significance levels.

Investment Equation

Tables 5.19 and 5.20 report the results of the difference GMM and the system GMM regressions of the investment equation, respectively, which correspond to the cross-section results in Table 5.12.[11] In these panel regressions, the ratio

10. The estimates were obtained in Stata using the one-step and two-step estimators implemented by Roodman (2006), including Windmeijer's (2005) finite-sample correction.

11. The estimates of the difference GMM regressions are based on a one-step estimator, and the system-GMM estimates are obtained using a two-step estimator including Windmeijer's (2005) finite-sample correction.

TABLE 5.17 Dynamic panel difference GMM estimations (Arellano-Bond procedure) (dependent variable: average annual growth of per capita GDP)

	Model 1	Model 2	Model 3	Model 4
Infrastructure aid/GDP ratio	–0.613	–0.552	–1.024	
	(0.461)	(0.482)	(0.780)	
Governance	–0.712	–0.648	–0.937	–0.249
	(0.540)	(0.428)	(0.589)	(0.450)
Infrastructure aid/GDP ratio × governance			0.218	
			(0.180)	
Infrastructure aid/GDP ratio × free				0.286
				(0.524)
Infrastructure aid/GDP ratio × partially free				–0.587
				(0.534)
Infrastructure aid/GDP ratio × not free				–0.292
				(0.448)
Investment ratio	0.186	0.160	0.137	0.153
	(0.085)***	(0.066)***	(0.053)**	(0.071)**
Initial GDP per capita (log)	–9.873	–9.226	–8.419	–9.022
	(2.260)***	(2.273)***	(3.076)***	(2.153)***
Openness	–0.011			–0.005
	(1.125)			(0.046)
Secondary school enrollment	–0.106	0.010	–0.114	–0.070
	(0.050)**	(0.070)	(0.048)**	(0.050)
Infant mortality (log)	–8.604	–7.744	–7.438	–5.917
	(2.949)***	(2.665)***	(2.143)***	(2.794)**
Inflation (log)	0.141	0.132	–0.046	–0.008
	(0.362)	(0.347)	(0.432)	(0.431)
Revolutions	–1.797	–1.536	–1.687	–1.474
	(0.817)**	(0.753)**	(0.783)**	(0.849)*
n	349	349	349	349
Number of groups	80	80	80	80
Number of instruments	70	66	76	79
Hansen *J*-test, *p*-value	0.405	0.313	0.317	0.293
Difference-in-Hansen test, *p*-values				
GMM-style IVs	0.338	0.393	0.232	0.521
Standard IVs	0.376	0.307	0.267	0.217
Test for AR(2)	0.583	0.579	0.349	0.637

SOURCES: Author's estimations using data from Rose (2004); Sala-i-Martin, Doppelhofer, and Miller (2004); Desmet, Ortuño-Ortin, and Wacziarg (2009); Heston, Summers, and Aten (2009); Marshall, Jaggers, and Gurr (2010); World Bank (2010); and OECD, Development Database on Aid Activities: CRS Online (various years).

NOTES: GMM: for generalized method of moments; IV: instrumental variable; AR(2): a second-order autocorrelation test in first differences. Robust standard errors are in parentheses. An empty cell indicates that the corresponding variable is not included in the model. Log means a variable is in logarithmic form. * indicates significant at the 10 percent level; ** indicates significant at the 5 percent level; *** indicates significant at the 1 percent level. Observations are five-year averages during the 1973–2002 horizon.

TABLE 5.18 Growth equation: Panel system GMM estimations (Blundell-Bond procedure) (dependent variable: average annual growth of per capita GDP)

	Model 1	Model 2	Model 3	Model 4
Infrastructure aid/GDP ratio	–0.305	–0.518	–0.637	
	(0.277)	(0.292)*	(0.555)	
Governance	0.356	–0.400	0.508	0.052
	(0.367)	(0.336)	(0.391)	(0.320)
Infrastructure aid/GDP ratio × governance			0.056	
			(0.211)	
Infrastructure aid/GDP ratio × free				–0.974
				(0.929)
Infrastructure aid/GDP ratio × partially free				–0.336
				(0.663)
Infrastructure aid/GDP ratio × not free				0.367
				(0.385)
Investment ratio	0.259	0.136	0.242	0.251
	(0.049)***	(0.058)**	(0.059)***	(0.061)***
Initial GDP per capita (log)	–2.536	–1.703	–2.674	–2.540
	(0.760)***	(0.807)**	(0.820)***	(1.010)**
Openness	–0.004			–0.015
	(0.011)			(0.008)**
Secondary school enrollment	0.018	–0.038	0.018	0.003
	(0.017)	(0.034)	(0.019)	(0.020)
Infant mortality (log)	–1.726	–2.441	–2.051	–2.289
	(0.872)**	(1.409)*	(1.034)**	(0.987)**
Initial inflation (log)	0.217	0.324	0.381	0.229
	(0.459)	(0.441)	(0.447)	(0.403)
Revolutions	–1.047	–1.748	–1.092	–1.548
	(0.655)	(0.564)**	(0.588)*	(0.730)**
n	435	435	435	435
Number of groups	81	81	81	81
Number of instruments	56	71	56	66
Hansen *J*-test	0.582	0.404	0.413	0.314
Difference-in-Hansen test, *p*-values				
GMM-style IVs (levels)	0.356	0.192	0.321	0.134
GMM-style IVs	0.443	0.136	0.446	0.421
Standard IVs	0.515	0.288	0.557	0.177
AR(2)	0.577	0.291	0.526	0.585

SOURCES: Author's estimations using data from Rose (2004); Sala-i-Martin, Doppelhofer, and Miller (2004); Desmet, Ortuño-Ortin, and Wacziarg (2009); Heston, Summers, and Aten (2009); Marshall, Jaggers, and Gurr (2010); World Bank (2010); and OECD, Development Database on Aid Activities: CRS Online (various years).

NOTES: GMM: generalized method of moments; IV: instrumental variable; AR(2): a second-order autocorrelation test in first differences. GMM-style instruments are collapsed and robust standard errors in parentheses. An empty cell indicates that the corresponding variable is not included in the model. Log means a variable is in logarithmic form. * indicates significant at the 10 percent level; ** indicates significant at the 5 percent level; *** indicates significant at the 1 percent level. Observations are five-year averages during the 1973–2002 horizon.

TABLE 5.19 Investment equation: Panel difference GMM estimations (Arellano-Bond procedure) (dependent variable: investment/GDP ratio)

	Model 1	Model 2	Model 3	Model 4
Economic aid/GDP ratio 0.725	1.032	0.673	0.826	
	(0.310)**	(0.417)	(0.246)***	(0.327)***
Democracy	–0.417	0.095	–0.285	–0.273
	(0.725)	(0.701)	(0.554)	(0.655)
Economic aid/GDP ratio × democracy		–0.136		
		(0.107)		
Economic aid/GDP ratio × partially free			–0.005	–0.136
			(0.316)	(0.267)
Economic aid/GDP ratio × not free			0.024	–0.074
			(0.246)	(0.304)
Initial GDP per capita (log)	5.048	4.972	4.456	
	(2.984)*	(2.956)*	(2.752)	
Initial policy	2.440	2.397	2.220	2.394
	(0.806)***	(0.841)***	(0.799)***	(0.810)***
Initial financial depth	–0.313	–0.313	–0.289	–0.301
	(0.080)***	(0.072)***	(0.070)***	(0.058)***
FDI/GDP ratio	0.767	0.701	0.659	0.731
	(0.229)***	(0.210)***	(0.181)***	(0.201)***
Initial inflation (log)	0.153	0.246	0.089	–0.197
	(0.527)	(0.529)	(0.518)	(0.252)
Revolutions	–1.515	–1.645	–1.620	–1.558
	(0.615)	(0.652)	(0.659)**	(0.700)**
n	281	281	281	281
Number of groups	80	80	80	80
Number of instruments	63	73	83	73
Hansen *J*-test	0.293	0.573	0.501	0.292
Difference-in-Hansen test, *p*-values				
GMM-style IVs (levels)	0.469	0.467	0.431	0.168
Standard IVs	0.237	0.528	0.446	0.275
AR(2)	0.709	0.567	0.588	0.842

SOURCES: Author's estimations using data from Rose (2004); Sala-i-Martin, Doppelhofer, and Miller (2004); Desmet, Ortuño-Ortin, and Wacziarg (2009); Heston, Summers, and Aten (2009); Marshall, Jaggers, and Gurr (2010); World Bank (2010); and OECD, Development Database on Aid Activities: CRS Online (various years).

NOTES: GMM: generalized method of moments; IV: instrumental variable; FDI: foreign direct investment; AR(2): a second-order autocorrelation test in first differences. Robust standard errors are in parentheses. An empty cell indicates that the corresponding variable is not included in the model. Log means a variable is in logarithmic form. * indicates significant at the 10 percent level; ** indicates significant at the 5 percent level; *** indicates significant at the 1 percent level. Observations are five-year averages during the 1973–2002 horizon.

TABLE 5.20 Investment equation: Panel system GMM estimations (Blundell-Bond procedure) (dependent variable: investment/GDP ratio)

	Model 1	Model 2	Model 3	Model 4
Economic aid/GDP ratio	0.388	–0.220	1.155	1.302
	(0.217)*	(0.459)	(0.561)**	(0.666)*
Democracy	–0.188	–0.779	–0.928	–1.123
	(0.347)	(0.614)	(0.428)**	(0.441)**
Economic aid/GDP ratio × democracy		0.196		
		(0.144)		
Economic aid/GDP ratio × partially free			–0.767	–0.925
			(0.479)	(0.530)*
Economic aid/GDP ratio × not free			–1.035	–1.325
			(0.557)*	(0.653)**
Initial GDP per capita (log)	3.254	3.271	3.427	2.668
	(0.896)**	(0.841)***	(0.908)***	(1.066)**
Initial policy	1.751	1.985	2.092	1.872
	(0.861)**	(0.906)**	(0.702)***	(0.718)**
Initial financial depth	–0.081	–0.066	–0.069	
	(0.033)**	(0.031)	(0.030)**	
FDI/GDP ratio	0.509	0.481	0.457	0.394
	(0.188)**	(0.179)***	(0.193)**	(0.210)*
Initial inflation (log)	0.614	0.604	0.851	1.161
	(0.374)	(0.385)	(0.532)	(0.444)**
Revolutions	–1.216	–1.311	–1.541	–1.364
	(0.587)**	(0.738)*	(0.649)**	(0.625)**
n	367	367	367	367
Number of groups	81	81	81	81
Number of instruments	72	77	79	74
Hansen *J*-test	0.270	0.318	0.270	0.379
Difference-in-Hansen test, *p*-values				
GMM-style IVs (levels)	0.230	0.112	0.103	0.159
GMM-style IVs	0.124	0.103	0.178	0.275
Standard IVs	0.234	0.213	0.190	0.292
AR(2)	0.191	0.289	0.300	0.269

SOURCES: Author's estimations using data from Rose (2004); Sala-i-Martin, Doppelhofer, and Miller (2004); Desmet, Ortuño-Ortin, and Wacziarg (2009); Heston, Summers, and Aten (2009); Marshall, Jaggers, and Gurr (2010); World Bank (2010); and OECD, Development Database on Aid Activities: CRS Online (various years).

NOTES: GMM: generalized method of moments; IV: instrumental variable; FDI: foreign direct investment; AR(2): a second-order autocorrelation test in first differences. Robust standard errors are in parentheses. An empty cell indicates that the corresponding variable is not included in the model. Log means a variable is in logarithmic form. * indicates significant at the 10 percent level; ** indicates significant at the 5 percent level; *** indicates significant at the 1 percent level. Observations are five-year averages during the 1973–2002 horizon.

of economic aid to GDP, governance, inflation, financial depth, and the FDI ratio are treated as endogenous and instrumented with the GMM-style instruments. Initial GDP per capita and revolutions are treated as predetermined. Constraints on the executive in 1900, having received independence after 1945, and geography are used as excluded instruments. In order to keep the number of instruments lower than the number of groups, in the system GMM regressions the GMM style instruments are collapsed.

The results are qualitatively similar to the cross-section results with a few exceptions. The first evidence to note is that the difference GMM regression estimate suggests that economic aid positively influences the investment ratio in recipient countries (Model 1 in Table 5.19). However, the positive system GMM estimate is statistically insignificant at conventional levels (Model 1 in Table 5.20). Second, the interaction of the ratio of economic aid to GDP with the governance variable is statistically insignificant in both the difference GMM and the system GMM regressions (Model 2 in Tables 5.19 and 5.20). Third the system GMM regression results provide some weak evidence of economic aid's positive effect on the ratio of investment to GDP in free (democratic) countries, whereas this effect could be negative for not free countries (Models 3 and 4 in Table 5.20). However, similar estimates from the difference GMM suggest that the impact of economic aid on the ratio of investment to GDP is positive and indifferent to the type of recipients' governance. Given that I collapsed the GMM-style instruments in the system GMM regressions to keep the number of instruments smaller than the number of groups (countries), the difference GMM regression results are preferred because collapsing reduces the statistical efficiency of panel GMM regressions (Roodman 2006, 2007). Overall, it seems that the panel regression results support the cross-section regression results with some exceptions.

Schooling Equation

The results of the difference GMM and the system GMM regressions with respect to the schooling equation are presented in Tables 5.21 and 5.22, respectively. These results correspond to the cross-section regression results reported in Table 5.14. In these panel regressions, the ratio of social aid to GDP, governance, ratio of public education expenditures to GDP, and infant mortality are treated as endogenous and instrumented with GMM-style instruments. All other covariates are treated as predetermined. Constraints on the executive in 1900, having received independence after 1945, and ethnic fractionalization are used as excluded instruments. Again, in order to control the number of instruments, in the system GMM regressions the GMM-style instruments are collapsed.

The results are qualitatively very similar to the cross-section regression results reported in Table 5.14. Overall, the panel results confirm that social aid has no statistically significant impact on secondary school enrollment. In addi-

TABLE 5.21 Schooling equation: Panel difference GMM estimations (Arellano-Bond procedure) (dependent variable: secondary school enrollment)

	Model 1	Model 2	Model 3	Model 4	Model 5
Social aid/GDP ratio	0.315	0.775	–0.185		
	(0.509)	(0.471)	(0.619)		
Governance	1.214	1.170	0.270	0.680	0.459
	(0.797)	(0.800)	(1.079)	(1.063)	(0.966)
Social aid/GDP ratio × governance			0.303		
			(0.209)		
Social aid/GDP ratio × free				1.579	1.351
				(1.143)	(1.188)
Social aid/GDP ratio × partially free				0.570	0.382
				(0.478)	(0.476)
Social aid/GDP ratio × not free				0.599	0.302
				(0.372)	(0.398)
Lagged secondary school enrollment	0.278	0.363	0.445	0.476	0.428
	(0.146)**	(0.131)***	(0.118)***	(0.124)***	(0.135)***
Initial GDP per capita (period)	8.570	8.042	8.677	8.459	9.377
	(2.810)***	(2.869)**	(2.735)***	(2.701)***	(2.640)***
Infant mortality	0.476	1.638	4.427	4.826	4.723
	(6.235)	(5.913)	(5.276)	(5.090)	(5.252)

Fertility	–2.748				–2.173
	(1.593)*				(1.509)
Urban	0.136	0.263	0.321	0.323	0.228
	(0.204)	(0.184)	(0.164)*	(0.166)*	(0.177)*
Education expenditures (percent of GDP)	2.576	2.240	2.006	1.632	1.756
	(0.892)***	(1.001)**	(0.937)**	(0.889)*	(0.814)*
Population under age 15	–0.454	–0.831	–0.827	–0.800	–0.518
	(0.422)	(0.389)**	(0.369)**	(0.363)**	(0.375)
n	301	301	301	301	301
Number of groups	78	78	78	78	78
Number of instruments	55	54	64	74	75
Hansen *J*-test	0.203	0.269	0.238	0.201	0.242
Difference-in-Hansen test, *p*-values					
GMM-style IVs	0.135	0.145	0.181	0.095	0.108
Standard IVs	0.178	0.203	0.159	0.194	0.161
AR(2)	0.853	0.811	0.622	0.530	0.514

SOURCES: Author's estimations using data from Rose (2004); Sala-i-Martin, Doppelhofer, and Miller (2004); Desmet, Ortuño-Ortin, and Wacziarg (2009); Heston, Summers, and Aten (2009); Marshall, Jaggers, and Gurr (2010); World Bank (2010); and OECD, Development Database on Aid Activities: CRS Online (various years).

NOTES: GMM: generalized method of moments; IV: instrumental variable; AR(2): a second-order autocorrelation test in first differences. Robust standard errors are in parentheses. An empty cell indicates that the corresponding variable is not included in the model. * indicates significant at the 10 percent level; ** indicates significant at the 5 percent level; *** indicates significant at the 1 percent level. Observations are five-year averages during the 1973–2002 horizon.

TABLE 5.22 Schooling equation: Panel system GMM estimations (Blundell-Bond procedure) (dependent variable: secondary school enrollment)

	Model 1	Model 2	Model 3	Model 4	Model 5
Social aid/GDP ratio	0.233	0.276	–1.047		
	(0.247)	(0.248)	(0.422)**		
Governance	–0.241	–0.284	–0.711	–1.327	–1.505
	(0.478)	(0.462)	(0.684)	(0.830)	(0.846)*
Social aid/GDP ratio × governance			0.391		
			(0.135)***		
Social aid/GDP ratio × free				1.080	1.288
				(1.213)	(1.291)
Social aid/GDP ratio × partially free				0.732	0.782
				(0.422)*	(0.441)*
Social aid/GDP ratio × not free				–0.785	–0.869
				(0.586)	(0.577)
Lagged average years of schooling	0.949	0.950	0.921	0.910	0.912
	(0.026)***	(0.025)***	(0.031)***	(0.039)***	(0.041)***
Initial GDP per capita (period)	2.717	2.925	2.476	2.659	3.088
	(1.193)**	(1.136)**	(1.258)*	(1.917)	(1.466)**
Infant mortality	6.372	6.038	5.617	5.710	6.730
	(2.677)***	(2.643)**	(2.369)**	(2.506)**	(3.111)**
Fertility	–0.209				–0.764
	(0.913)				(1.143)

Urban	0.018	0.015	0.026	0.008	–0.001
	(0.033)	(0.035)	(0.032)	(0.043)	(0.041)
Education expenditures (percent of GDP)	1.386	1.269	1.495	1.696	1.641
	(0.517)**	(0.523)**	(0.559)***	(0.759)**	(0.766)**
Population under age 15	–0.496	–0.512	–0.520	–0.644	–0.545
	(0.207)**	(0.180)***	(0.182)***	(0.187)***	(0.189)***
n	382	382	382	382	382
Number of groups	79	79	79	79	79
Number of instruments	79	78	74	52	53
Hansen *J*-test	0.578	0.591	0.559	0.366	0.345
Difference-in-Hansen test, *p*-values					
GMM-style IVs (levels)	0.327	0.319	0.547	0.274	0.236
GMM-style IVs	0.541	0.532	0.119	0.183	0.184
Standard IVs	0.421	0.478	0.724	0.278	0.263
AR(2)	0.395	0.402	0.342	0.362	0.350

SOURCES: Author's estimations using data from Rose (2004); Sala-i-Martin, Doppelhofer, and Miller (2004); Desmet, Ortuño-Ortin, and Wacziarg (2009); Heston, Summers, and Aten (2009); Marshall, Jaggers, and Gurr (2010); World Bank (2010); and OECD, Development Database on Aid Activities: CRS Online (various years).

NOTES: GMM: generalized method of moments; IV: instrumental variable; AR(2): a second-order autocorrelation test in first differences. Robust standard errors are in parentheses. An empty cell indicates that the corresponding variable is not included in the model. * indicates significant at the 10 percent level; ** indicates significant at the 5 percent level; *** indicates significant at the 1 percent level. Observations are five-year averages during the 1973–2002 horizon.

tion, there is no evidence of a positive or negative link between the quality of democratic governance and secondary school enrollment. At the same time, the system GMM panel regression results suggest that social aid's impact on secondary schooling is influenced by the level of governance (Model 3 in Table 5.22). The estimated coefficients for social aid and its interaction with governance are −1.047 and 0.391, respectively. These coefficients are jointly, as well as individually, significant at conventional levels. This suggests that the marginal impact of social aid on school enrollment changes with the level of governance. This marginal effect can be calculated as $-1.047 + 0.391 \times$ governance. Based on this, one can suggest that social aid has a statistically significant reductive effect on school enrollment when the governance score is very low. However, once the governance score is equal to 3 or higher, the marginal impact of social aid on school enrollment turns positive. The difference GMM coefficients have similar signs but are statistically insignificant. Also, the interactions of social aid with the three governance categories are insignificant in both procedures. Much as in the case of the cross-section results, the panel GMM regressions suggest that schooling is persistent and that richer countries are likely to have higher school enrollment rates. One striking difference is that the panel results suggest that there is a significant positive relationship between public education expenditures and schooling. Also, the panel results suggest that the share of the population under age 15 has a significant negative effect on school enrollment.

Summarizing the empirical results reported in this chapter, it is worth noting that disaggregation of total aid into subcomponents shows that economic aid is likely to positively affect economic growth in recipient countries through its impact on domestic investment. However, these results also suggest that there is no significant link between social aid and schooling in aid-recipient countries. Are these findings consistent with the theoretical and empirical literature? How can one explain these results? The next chapter briefly summarizes the findings of the study and then addresses these questions.

6 Conclusion

This study has examined the aid–growth relationship by disaggregating total aid into economic, social, and other aid components. The main assumption in this study is that only the economic and social aid components are likely to affect economic growth in recipient countries. These two aid components account for roughly two-thirds of total aid and are intended by donors to build additional physical and human capital in recipient countries. Other aid components (for example, food and emergency aid) account for one-third of total aid and are primarily intended for consumption purposes. The analytical framework of the study differentiates three possible impact channels in the aid–growth relationship. The first impact channel is one in which economic aid, including ODA to the production and economic infrastructure sectors, influences economic growth through its impact on domestic investment (capital accumulation). Next, the part of economic aid that goes to economic infrastructure may directly affect economic growth by improving the economic infrastructure (for example, roads), which helps to reduce transaction costs. Finally, social aid, including ODA to the education and health sectors, may affect economic growth by building additional human capital. The analysis also examined whether the level of governance in recipient countries is important for the effectiveness of aid.

The study addressed the problem of endogeneity in the aid–growth relationship using instrumentation strategy and GMM panel regressions. In the context of cross-section regression analysis, it was addressed by constructing a complicated instrument for aggregate aid and its components. This complicated instrument was based mainly on donor-related rather than recipient-specific factors.[1] To address the problem of the endogeneity of democratic governance, the level of constraints on the executive in 1900, coded from the Polity IV dataset (Marshall, Jaggers, and Curr 2010), and a dummy for countries that obtained independence after 1945 were used as instruments. The validity of these

1. The instrumentation strategy used in this study improves on and extends the approach initially suggested by Rajan and Subramanian (2008).

instruments was tested by applying a series of overidentification and exclusion restrictions tests. The study also stated the problem of simultaneity—the notion that investment, schooling, and economic growth are jointly determined in the analytical framework. To cope with this problem, a simultaneous-equations approach was implemented that allows one to simultaneously solve the growth, investment, and schooling equations using the 3SLS estimator. In this framework, instrumentation for aid components is done at the first stage, the investment and schooling equations are estimated at the second (intermediate) stage, and the growth equation is estimated at the third stage. The cross-section estimates based on simultaneous system equations, including the instruments for aid components and governance, are the preferred results. The dynamic panel GMM results, which support the main cross-section results, are provided as additional checks.

The analysis of aid allocation reveals that historical factors and donors' geopolitical and commercial interests are important determinants of donors' aid allocation decisions. The aid allocation decisions are also somewhat affected by recipients' needs at the eligibility as well as the aid allocation stages. The analysis of aggregate aid allocation suggests that recipients with better democratic governance have a higher probability of being eligible to receive foreign aid. They also receive relatively higher amounts of aid per capita at the aggregate level. Concerning the donors' sectoral aid allocation decisions, the donor countries seem to provide relatively more aid per capita for social uses to partially free and free countries than to not free countries. There is virtually no difference in per capita aid allocated for economic uses among these three groups of countries. The results also reveal some important differences among individual donors' aid allocation policies. For example, geopolitical and strategic considerations seem more important to the United States than to the Nordic countries. These findings were employed to construct complicated instruments for different aid categories in an aid effectiveness analysis.

The analysis of the aid–growth relationship shows that there is no significant relationship between aggregate aid and per capita GDP growth. The examination of the disaggregated aid–growth relationship suggests that the direct impact of aid to economic infrastructure on per capita GDP growth is insignificant. However, further analysis shows that economic aid has a significant positive impact on economic growth through its positive impact on physical capital accumulation. The 3SLS regression results indicate that the ratio of investment to GDP has a positive causal impact on the long-term average growth rates of per capita GDP, with an estimated coefficient of 0.12. In turn, the 3SLS regression results for the investment equation also show a statistically significant positive relationship between economic aid and domestic investment, with an estimated coefficient of 2.17. Combining these two results, it would be possible to claim that a 1 percentage point increase in the ratio of economic aid to GDP increases the long-run per capita growth rate by 0.27 (2.17×0.123) percent. The results of cross-section investment regressions are qualitatively supported by the results of dynamic panel (both difference GMM and system GMM) regressions.

These findings are consistent with the theoretical and empirical literature. Rajan and Subramanian (2008) consider the impact of aid on growth in a neoclassical growth framework. Assuming that aid helps recipients only in physical capital accumulation and has no effect on productivity, they conclude that "an upper limit for the impact of aid on growth would be about 0.2–0.25% per year for every 1 percentage point increase in the received aid to GDP ratio" (Rajan and Subramanian 2008, 664).[2] The empirical findings in this study are very close to the upper limit of the theoretical prediction of the impact of aggregate aid on economic growth provided by Rajan and Subramanian (2008). One important difference is that they assume that all foreign aid is invested. However, one can argue that it is not plausible to assume that all foreign aid is invested because considerable shares of ODA are intended for consumption (for example, for food aid), technical assistance, and other similar purposes. It is more plausible to assume that all or most of economic aid is invested. Therefore, my finding is more consistent with the predictions of the neoclassical growth model.

Further, these results are consistent with those of past research that has consistently found that foreign aid stimulates investment. For example, Levy (1987) finds that an increase of 1 percentage point in the ratio of aid to GDP is associated with an increase of 0.86–1.08 percentage points in the ratio of investment to GDP. More recently Hansen and Tarp (2001), in a cross-sectional study including 56 of the least developed countries, estimated that the coefficient for the impact of aid on the investment ratio is 0.71. Another study by Dollar and Easterly (1999) suggested that the relationship between foreign aid and investment is heterogeneous across countries. Furthermore, these results are also consistent with a broad empirical literature that suggests that economic growth, especially in less developed economies, is primarily driven by capital accumulation (Chow 1993; Krugman 1994; Young 1995; Collins and Bosworth 1996).

The magnitude of the estimated coefficient for the impact of the ratio of economic aid to GDP on investment suggests that public investment financed by aid has significant spillover effects. This might be surprising at first look, because economic theory suggests that public investment may cause a crowding-out effect by reducing the loanable funds available for private investment and by distorting relative prices. However, public investment financed by foreign aid does not compete with the private sector for domestic funds. Most households in less developed countries live below the subsistence level, and there is no or very limited domestic (personal or public) savings to finance public and private investment. Therefore, foreign aid intended to finance investment projects in productive sectors such as agriculture and economic infrastructure such

2. For details, see Appendix C in Rajan and Subramanian (2008, 664).

as roads might help increase the ratio of investment to GDP in aid recipient countries. Further, the stock of public roads, bridges, communication systems, and other infrastructure is essential to the development of an efficient private sector. There is broad evidence suggesting that investment in public infrastructure (roads, bridges, and so on) reduces the cost of capital and increases the marginal productivity of private capital, which, in turn, crowds in private investment (Aschauer 1989, 2000; Fan 2008). Therefore, economic development aid might encourage both domestic and foreign private investors to invest more in the country.

The results concerning the impact of social aid on economic growth through its impact on secondary school enrollment are not as expected. The results of a system of simultaneous-equation regressions suggest that an increase of 1 percent in secondary school enrollment leads to a 0.05 percent increase in the long-run rate of per capita GDP growth. However, one cannot link this positive impact with aid to the social sector based on the cross-section results, which suggest that there is no statistically positive relationship between the ratio of social aid to GDP and secondary school enrollment. These results remain qualitatively unchanged when primary school enrollment or average years of schooling is used as the dependent variable (not reported). At the same time, the system GMM panel regression results suggest that social aid's impact on secondary schooling is positive when the governance score is equal to 3 or higher. However, the difference GMM results do not support this finding.

There are some contextual explanations. The problems with the quality of schooling data are well documented (Bennell 2002; Dreber, Nunnenkamp, and Thiele 2008). The evidence suggests that data on schooling include a lot of noise and measurement error. For example, a 2006 edition of the *Index of Economic Freedom,* sponsored by the Heritage Foundation and the *Wall Street Journal,* report that government data on education in the state of Lagos in Nigeria underestimates the number of children in school by 24 percent. Similar problems were observed in Ghana, India, and Kenya (Tooley and Dixon 2006). Therefore, one may argue that the measurement error may have affected the regression results. It can also be argued that using data on social aid, which includes aid to health, water, and sanitation in addition to education, produced imprecise estimates with large standard errors. In fact, the dynamic panel estimates of the impact of social aid on school enrollment were mainly positive but statistically insignificant. However, extensive empirical evidence now shows that factors related to health and drinking water have a significant impact on school enrollment. Miguel and Kremer (2004), for instance, have shown that a deworming program substantially improved both health and school participation in rural areas of Kenya.

Further, both cross-section and panel regressions reveal significant inertia in secondary school enrollment. The initial school enrollment is highly significant and has strong explanatory power, causing some of the other covariates included in the analysis to be insignificant. This finding is consistent with previous literature and applies to both primary school enrollment and average years of schooling (Bennell 2002; Clemens 2004; Dreber, Nunnenkamp, and Thiele 2008). In this regard, Clemens (2004, 1), summarizing a broad micro-level literature on education, concludes that "economic conditions and slowly-changing parental education levels determine children's school enrollment to a greater degree than education policy interventions." If one accepts this conclusion, foreign aid can do very little to increase school enrollment in developing countries without long-term improvements in economic incentives for education. Foreign aid, if spent efficiently, can help to increase the number of schools available. But even with readily available schools, it cannot increase enrollment if the private expected benefit of additional schooling remains relatively low. The private benefits of education depend mainly on labor market expectations and are limited to a greater extent by the pace of economic development (Clemens 2004). The problems of public education for the poor in developing countries are well documented by many studies. For example, Watkins (2000, 230) suggests that "there is little or no value in attending school. Under these circumstances, it is not difficult to see why many poor households regard spending on (public) education as a bad use of scarce resources." Drèze and Sen (2002) also observed similar evidence in India.

This study also considered the possibility that the impact of foreign aid on development outcomes might depend on democratic governance in the recipient countries. Some argue that by providing institutionalized checks on government, democratic governance will encourage them to use development assistance more productively. In this regard, Svensson (2000a) and Kosack (2003) find that foreign aid is positively associated with economic growth and quality of life in democracies but detrimental in nondemocratic (developing) countries receiving aid. However, the findings of this study do not provide adequate support for the notion that the impact of aid depends on democratic governance. It seems that economic development, at least at the early stages, can be promoted even under pro-market, nondemocratic regimes if they can secure property rights as a matter of policy choice, not of political constraints, and if they allow human and physical capital accumulation to start the process (Glaeser et al. 2004). On the other hand, even in some democratic developing countries, elites may pursue their private interests using rent-seeking and corruption, which may lead to inefficient use of foreign aid and skewed income distribution (Bjórnskov 2010).

The findings of this study should be interpreted with due caution because disaggregation of total aid into different categories could be subject to fungibility. Rajan and Subramanian (2008) argue that this fungibility may imply that how well aid is translated into growth may depend not on the specific purpose for which aid is given but on how efficiently the recipient government uses all development assistance. There is a broad literature on aid fungibility, which identifies two types of aid fungibility: (1) fungibility in the development or foreign aid context refers to the recipients' ability to circumvent donor-imposed restrictions and spend some amount of targeted aid on other programs, and (2) fungibility in the public finance context refers to the ability of an aid recipient to replace its own expenditures with aid transfers and to transform some portion of targeted aid into pure income or income-generating resources that can be spent in the way the recipient chooses (Devarajan and Swarup 1998).

The literature also agrees that different categories of foreign aid are subject to fungibility at different levels. Project aid, which is given to finance individual projects in the production, infrastructure, and social sectors, is less prone to fungibility than is program aid, which is channeled directly through the budget of the recipient's government, with the funds provided not separable from the government's budget (White 1998). Rajan and Subramanian (2008, 655) mentioned that "one category of aid that might avoid the fungibility problem is technical assistance because of the manner in which it is provided." McGillivray and Morrissey (2000) argued that the part of aid that does not go through the recipient's budget accounts is not appropriate for analyzing fungibility. A more recent study by Van de Sijpe (2010) provides a rigorous analysis of the issue and finds a low level of aid fungibility. Given these arguments, one can definitely argue that aid for social uses is less prone to fungibility because technical assistance is the dominant modality in education and health sectors. For example, about two-thirds of education aid is provided in the form of technical assistance (Dreber, Nunnenkamp, and Thiele 2008). In a same manner, most economic aid is provided through specific investment projects to build and maintain roads, bridges, irrigation networks, and so forth.

Therefore, it can be argued that the concerns related to aid fungibility will not significantly alter the results obtained in this study. Nevertheless, a few additional empirical exercises (the results of which are not reported) were conducted to address this problem. First, following Mishra and Newhouse (2009), this study replaces economic aid with social aid in the investment equation to assess whether there is something specific about economic aid that affects investment or whether economic aid is replaceable with social aid. The results show no significant causal link between social aid and the investment ratio, suggesting that there are significant differences among different categories of aid. Then economic and social aid, one by one, are directly included in the growth equation. The results of the reduced-form regressions show that, as expected, economic aid has a significant positive impact on per capita growth, with an estimated coefficient of 0.41, which is slightly higher than the estimate obtained from a system of simultaneous equations. On the other hand, as expected, the estimated coefficient for the impact of aid for social uses is statistically insignificant. An alternative specification would simultaneously include both economic and social aid variables in the growth equation. However, collinearity is a serious problem for this specification because all aid variables share a common cause (that is, aid is provided because a recipient country is poor). This is an interesting area for future research.

Appendixes

A Development Thinking and Foreign Aid

TABLE A.1 Overview of trends in the relationship between development thinking and foreign aid

Objectives	Development theories and models	Policies and strategies	Roles of foreign aid
Early 1950s to late 1960s: Economic growth External equilibrium Employment	"Big push," "take-off," and stages of growth, balanced growth (Nurkse 1953) Economic dualism and the role of agriculture (Fei and Ranis 1964) Intersectoral structure and patterns of growth (Chenery 1960; Kuznets 1966) Harrod-Domar and two-gap models (Chenery and Strout 1966)	Industrialization through import substitution Social and infrastructure investment with an emphasis on the urban sector Fine-tuning and appropriate prices "Balanced growth" between agriculture and industry Regional integration	Serve as source of capital to trigger economic growth through higher investment based on a belief in government capacity to use aid efficiently Remove investment–savings and import–export constraints and support the "balanced growth" strategy
Early 1970s to early 1980s: Economic growth Poverty alleviation Employment Income distribution External equilibrium	Integrated rural and agricultural development (Johnston and Kilby 1975) Role of nonfarm employment (Hymer and Resnick 1969) Importance of demographic variables and rural-urban migration (Harris and Todaro 1970) Trade-off between output, employment, income distribution, and poverty (Little and Mirrlees 1974)	Unimodal strategy in rural development, comprehensive employment strategies, "redistribution with growth," and "basic needs fulfillment"	Support the "redistribution with growth" and "basic needs fulfillment" strategies Make poverty alleviation a major criterion for aid allocation Emphasize integrated rural development

Early 1980s to late 1990s: Macroeconomic stabilization Structural adjustment External and internal equilibrium Liberalization and deregulation Human development (education and health)	Endogenous growth (Lucas 1988) Role of human capital (Mankiw, Romer, and Weil 1992) Trade and growth (Frankel and Romer 1999) Stabilization and structural adjustment (Fischer 1993; Agenor and Montiel 1996) General equilibrium models based on social accounting matrix (Dervis, de Melo, and Robinson 1982) Living standards measurement surveys (Deaton 1997)	Stabilization and structural adjustment, outward orientation, privatization, deregulation, and liberalization Reliance on markets and minimization of the role of government	Support developing countries to service their external debt Provide incentives for developing and transition countries to implement macroeconomic stabilization and structural adjustment policies through conditionality
Mid-1990s and early 2000s: Pro-poor growth and poverty reduction Good governance and institution-building Millennium Development Goals Global health (HIV/AIDs and other communicable diseases) Global security and anti-terrorism	Role of institutions in development and endogeneity of policies (North 1990; World Bank 1993) Implications of information economics for development (Hoff, Braverman, and Stiglitz 1993) Political economy of development and the role of institutions (Acemoglu, Johnson, and Robinson 2001)	Poverty reduction strategies Participation and ownership and public–private partnerships in decisionmaking Decentralization of governance and community-driven development Promoting peer monitoring, group lending, and microfinance institutions Policies to enhance security and postconflict development	Promote good governance and policies through selectivity Enhance security Support poverty reduction Promote MDGs Provide assistance to cure communicable diseases and pandemics Support agriculture and global food security

(*continued*)

TABLE A.1 Continued

Objectives	Development theories and models	Policies and strategies	Roles of foreign aid
Reduced vulnerability to external shocks such as global food and financial crises	Growth–inequality–poverty nexus, sources of pro-poor growth (Ravallion and Chen 2003) Security and development (Krueger and Malečková 2003; Abadie 2005) Randomized experiments in development evaluation (Duflo and Kremer 2005) Reviving agriculture for development (World Bank 2007)	Focus on governance and performance-based aid allocation	

SOURCES: Author's summation based on the sources cited in the table and also on Hjertholm and White (2000); Thorbecke (2000); and Kanbur (2006).

NOTE: Entries are not exhaustive but list main features; of course there are exceptions.

B Lists of Donors and Aid Recipients

Donors

Australia, Austria, Belgium, Canada, Denmark, Finland, France, Germany, Greece, Ireland, Italy, Japan, Netherlands, New Zealand, Norway, Portugal, Spain, Sweden, Switzerland, United Kingdom, United States

Aid Recipients

Algeria, Angola, Argentina, Bangladesh, Barbados, Belize, Benin, Bhutan, Bolivia, Botswana, Brazil, Burkina Faso, Burundi, Cambodia, Cameroon, Cape Verde, Central African Republic, Chad, Chile, China, Colombia, Comoros, Democratic Republic of Congo, Republic of Congo, Costa Rica, Côte d'Ivoire, Croatia, Cyprus, Djibouti, Dominican Republic, Ecuador, Egypt, El Salvador, Equatorial Guinea, Eritrea, Ethiopia, Fiji, Gabon, Gambia, Ghana, Grenada, Guatemala, Guinea, Guinea Bissau, Guyana, Haiti, Honduras, India, Indonesia, Iran, Jamaica, Jordan, Kenya, Korea Republic, Laos, Lebanon, Lesotho, Liberia, Libya, Madagascar, Malawi, Malaysia, Maldives, Mali, Mauritania, Mauritius, Mexico, Morocco, Mozambique, Namibia, Nepal, Nicaragua, Niger, Nigeria, Oman, Pakistan, Panama, Papua New Guinea, Paraguay, Peru, Philippines, Rwanda, Senegal, Sierra Leone, Singapore, South Africa, Sri Lanka, Sudan, Suriname, Swaziland, Syria, Tanzania, Thailand, Togo, Tonga, Trinidad and Tobago, Tunisia, Turkey, Uganda, Uruguay, Venezuela, Yemen, Zambia, Zimbabwe

C Definitions and Sources of Regression Variables

TABLE C.1 Definitions and sources of regression variables

Variable	Definition	Source
Real economic growth	Annual average growth rate of real GDP per capita	Heston, Summers, and Aten (2009)
Investment ratio	Annual average ratio of investment to GDP	Heston, Summers, and Aten (2009)
Secondary school enrollment	Gross secondary school enrollment, the ratio (percentage) of total enrollment, regardless of age, to the population of the age group that officially corresponds to those receiving secondary school education	World Bank (2010)
Ratio of aid to GDP	Ratio of net aggregate official development assistance (ODA) in current US dollars to GDP in current US dollars	OECD, Development Database on Aid from DAC Members: DAC Online (various years)
Ratio of economic aid to GDP	Ratio of ODA for economic uses in current US dollars to GDP in current US dollars	OECD, Development Database on Aid Activities: CRS Online (various years)
Ratio of infrastructure aid to GDP	Ratio of ODA to economic infrastructure in current US dollars to GDP in current US dollars	OECD, Development Database on Aid Activities: CRS Online (various years)
Ratio of social aid to GDP	Ratio of ODA for social uses in current US dollars to GDP in current US dollars	OECD, Development Database on Aid Activities: CRS Online (various years)
Governance (democracy)	Freedom House's political rights and civil liberties indicators combined and then reversed symmetrically, resulting in a new democracy variable with a scales from 1 to 7	Freedom House (2009)

TABLE C.1 Continued

Variable	Definition	Source
Categories free, partially free, and not free	Freedom House's classification based on average combined political rights and civil liberties ratings: free = countries with a combined original (not reversed) ratings average of 1.0–2.5; partly free = those with a combined original ratings average of 3.0–5.0; not free = those with a combined original ratings average of 5.5–7.0	Freedom House (2009)
Constraints on executives in 1900	Extent of institutional constraints on the decisionmaking powers of the executive branch; degree of checks and balances between the various parts of the government coded on a 7-point scale ranging from unlimited executive authority (1) to executive parity or subordination (7)	Polity IV database (Marshall, Jaggers, and Gurr 2010)
Initial policy	Sachs-Warner trade policy indicator as updated by Wacziarg and Welch (2003)	Wasciarg and Welch (2003)
Initial GDP per capita	Log of per capita GDP at the beginning of the relevant time period	World Bank (2010)
Infant mortality	Number of infants per 1,000 live births in a given time period who died before reaching 1 year of age	World Bank (2010)
Life expectancy	Number of years a newborn infant would live if the patterns of mortality prevailing at the time of its birth were to stay the same throughout its life	World Bank (2010)
Life expectancy in 1960	Life expectancy in 1960s	Sala-i-Martin, Doppelhofer, and Miller (2004)
Financial depth	Money and quasi-money (Model 2) as a percentage of GDP	World Bank (2010)
Ratio of foreign direct investment (FDI) to GDP (%)	Ratio of FDI to GDP	World Bank (2010)
Inflation	Average annual consumer price index–based inflation for the beginning of the relevant time period	World Bank (2010)
Average inflation (1960–90)	Average inflation in 1960–90	Sala-i-Martin, Doppelhofer, and Miller (2004)

(*continued*)

TABLE C.1 Continued

Variable	Definition	Source
Openness	Openness in current prices	Heston, Summers, and Aten (2009)
Initial openness	Average openness measure in 1965–74	Sala-i-Martin, Doppelhofer, and Miller (2004)
Public education expenditures, percentage of GDP	Public expenditure on education, including current and capital public expenditure on education	World Bank (2010)
Malaria risk in 1960s	Malaria prevalence in 1966	Sala-i-Martin, Doppelhofer, and Miller (2004)
Coastal population density in 1960s	Coastal population density in 1960s	
Population under age 15	Population ages 0–14 (percentage of total)	World Bank (2010)
Political similarity	Similarity of preferences among pairs of states, proxied using the Affinity of Nations index, based on Spearman rank-order correlations of roll-call voting patterns in the UN General Assembly	Gartzke (2010)
Colony	Dummy for pairs that ever had a colonial relationship	Rose (2004)
Current colony	Dummy for pairs that currently (recently) have (had) a colonial relationship	Rose (2004)
Common language	Dummy for pairs that have a common language	CIA (2011)
Colony of Portugal	Dummy for countries that ever had a colonial relationship with Portugal	CIA (2011)
Population ratio (log)	Logarithm ratio of population of donor relative to recipient	World Bank (2010)
Initial share of agriculture in GDP, percent	Share of agricultural value added in total GDP for the early 1970s or for the closest year for which data are available	World Bank (2010)
Initial donor exports to recipient country	Log of average donor exports for 1973–77	IMF (2006)
Initial share of rural population	Share of the rural population in the total population for the early 1970s or for the closest year for which data are available	World Bank (2010)
Primary schooling in 1960s	Primary schooling in 1960	Sala-i-Martin, Doppelhofer, and Miller (2004)
Initial ratio of physicians to population (1970s)	Number of physicians per 1,000 people for the early 1970s or for the closest year for which data are available	World Bank (2010)

TABLE C.1 Continued

Variable	Definition	Source
Initial access to drinking water	Share of people with access to improved drinking-water sources for the early 1970s or for the closest years for which data are available	World Bank (2010)
Initial fertility in 1970s	Expected fertility rate for the early 1970s or for the closest year for which data are available	World Bank (2010)
Geography	Absolute latitude	Sala-i-Martin, Doppelhofer, and Miller (2004)
Ethnic fractionalization	Likelihood that two people chosen at random will be from different ethnic groups	Desmet, Ortuño-Ortin, and Wacziarg (2009)

NOTES: In the cross-section regressions, the averages are for 1973–2002. In the dynamic panel regressions, the averages are from the relevant five-year periods. Initial values are for the beginning of the relevant time period or for the closest year for which data are available.

D Descriptive Summary Statistics

TABLE D.1 Descriptive summary statistics

Variable	Mean	Standard deviation	Minimum	Maximum
Real annual per capita GDP growth	0.971	2.037	–5.062	7.188
Ratio of investment to GDP	17.807	10.509	3.349	57.287
Secondary school enrollment in 1998–2002	50.281	28.209	5.948	104.837
Secondary school enrollment in 1973–77	26.557	19.216	1.635	80.300
Primary school enrollment in 1960	61.595	30.129	5.000	100.000
Ratio of aggregate aid to GDP	6.459	7.444	0.049	42.468
Ratio of fitted aggregate aid to GDP	6.351	6.692	–6.851	43.648
Ratio of economic aid to GDP	2.279	2.383	0.011	11.849
Ratio of fitted economic aid to GDP	2.241	2.000	–1.814	13.507
Ratio of aid to economic infrastructure to GDP	1.087	1.147	0.006	6.014
Ratio of fitted aid to economic infrastructure to GDP	1.068	1.023	–0.923	7.363
Ratio of social aid to GDP	1.592	1.894	0.009	10.592
Ratio of fitted social aid to GDP	1.591	1.489	–1.916	5.580
Governance (democracy) score (reversed)	3.669	1.348	1.450	6.967
Executive constraints in 1900	3.383	2.321	1.000	7.000
Initial level of GDP per capita	7.861	0.811	5.992	9.627
Initial openness	0.535	0.348	0.067	2.461
Financial depth	24.335	13.085	8.532	84.778
Ratio of foreign aid to GDP	1.853	2.180	–0.083	14.145
Consumer price index–based average inflation (log)	2.709	0.624	1.464	5.733
Average inflation in 1960–90	14.374	15.695	3.267	88.984
Coastal population density in 1965	96.4	352.6	0.0	3082.0
Life expectancy in 2000 (log)	3.870	0.796	1.253	5.013
Life expectancy in 1960	47.5	9.2	31.5	68.8
Malaria risk in 1960s	0.493	0.443	0.000	1.000
Public education expenditures (percent of GDP)	3.270	1.336	0.583	6.595
Share of population under age 15, percent	43.046	4.528	26.119	49.692
Geography (absolute latitude)	16.202	11.224	0.228	41.202
Revolutions	0.237	0.238	0.000	1.267
Ethnic fractionalization	0.531	0.255	0.002	0.930

SOURCES: Author's estimations using data from OECD, Development Database on Aid Activities: CRS Online (various years), and OECD, Development Database on Aid from DAC Members: DAC Online (various years); Rose (2004); Sala-i-Martin, Doppelhofer, and Miller (2004); Desmet, Ortuño-Ortin, and Wacziar (2009); Heston, Summers, and Aten (2009); Marshall, Jaggers, and Gurr (2010); and World Bank (2010).

NOTE: Log means a variable is in logarithmic form.

E General Characteristics of Political Rights Scores and Civil Liberties Scores

TABLE E.1 General characteristics of political rights scores

Score	Description	Examples of countries
1	Country has a fully competitive electoral process with free and fair elections and competitive political parties; opposition has actual power and plays an important role.	Barbados, Bulgaria, Cape Verde, Costa Rica, Grenada, Hungary
2	Country's political rights are the same as ranking 1, but such factors as political corruption, political discrimination against minorities, and foreign military influence on the political process may be present and weaken the quality of political freedom.	Bolivia, Botswana, Brazil, Chile, Croatia, El Salvador, Ghana, India, Jamaica, Mexico, Namibia, Peru, Senegal
3	Country's political rights are characterized by less effective enforcement of competitive election process than ranking 1 or 2.	Albania, Argentina, Benin, Ecuador, Honduras, Indonesia, Macedonia
4	Country's political rights are the same as ranking 3, but government may have been selected outside the public view by various faction leaders.	Bangladesh, Bosnia-Herzegovina, Burkina-Faso, Colombia, Djibouti, Georgia, Guatemala
5	Country has no effective electoral process in place; there is a struggle for consensus among a variety of political, ethnic, and other groups in society.	Bahrain, Central African Republic, Comoros, Ethiopia, Malaysia, Russia
6	No competitive electoral processes are allowed, and country is ruled by a one-party dictatorship, religious hierarchy, military junta, or autocrat; however, leaders may respond to certain popular (cultural, religious, and ethnic) desires.	Afghanistan, Algeria, Bhutan, Burundi, Cambodia, Chad, Congo, Côte d'Ivoire, Iran, Jordan, Lebanon, Liberia, Pakistan, Qatar, Somalia, Tajikistan
7	Political rights are absent or virtually nonexistent, and power is controlled by political despots only.	Burma, China, Cuba, Eritrea, Iraq, North Korea, Libya, Rwanda, Sudan

SOURCE: Author's compilation using Freedom House (2009).

TABLE E.2 General characteristics of civil liberties scores

Score	Description	Examples of countries
1	Country provides full freedom of expression, assembly, association, education, and religion and is distinguished by an established and generally equitable rule of law.	Barbados, Chile, Kiribati, Marshall Islands, Slovenia, Uruguay
2	Country's status is similar to ranking 1, but there are deficiencies in the implementation of some aspects of civil liberties.	Belize, Benin, Bulgaria, Cape Verde, Costa Rica, Guyana, Latvia, South Africa
3	There are some elements of censorship in the press and some restrictions with respect to assembly, association, and religion.	Albania, Argentina, Bolivia, Brazil, Ecuador, Fiji, Ghana, India, Lesotho, Mali, Namibia, Tanzania
4	The press is strongly censored, free speech and other civil liberties are limited, and torture may be used.	Bangladesh, Burkina Faso, Colombia, Gabon, Indonesia, Kenya, Niger
5	There is little or no free press, legal authorities have apparently extensive control over social order, and political prisoners are being held.	Algeria, Angola, Chad, Djibouti, Ethiopia, Guinea, Kazakhstan, Lebanon, Morocco, Pakistan
6	There are severely restricted rights of expression and association; a few civil liberties, such as some religious and social freedoms; and some highly restricted private business activity.	Belarus, Cameron, China, Haiti, Iran, Laos, Liberia, Qatar, Uzbekistan, Vietnam, Zimbabwe
7	There are virtually no civil liberties and an overwhelming and justified fear of repression based on politics and ethnicity.	Burma, Cuba, Iraq, North Korea, Libya, Saudi Arabia, Somalia, Syria, Turkmenistan

SOURCE: Author's compilation using Freedom House (2009).

F Governance and Rent Extraction–Efficiency Trade-off in Aid Allocation

The main objective of this model is to characterize the optimal rent extraction–efficiency trade-off faced by the donors (principals) when designing their aid allocation policies and develop testable hypotheses for econometric estimation. I do this through the following steps. First, I describe the donors' motives in providing and allocating aid and the set of allocations that the donors can achieve despite the information gap. Any donor making an aid allocation decision considers an impact to be produced and a transfer of aid flows. To characterize those allocations one needs to describe donors' objective function, a set of incentive compatibility constraints, and participation constraints. Incentive compatibility constraints are due to information asymmetry, while participation constraints are required to ensure that recipients are willing to participate in the agreement. Incentive and participation constraints give the set of feasible allocations. Second, once this characterization is achieved, I proceed to normative analysis and optimize donors' objective function within the set of incentive-feasible allocations. Then, I investigate the impact of improvements of the donors' information system on the optimal aid allocation.

In doing this, I implicitly apply the following assumptions, which are standard for principal–agent models (Laffont and Martimort 2002). First, I assume that donors and recipients are both fully rational economic agents and maximize their own utility. Second, I assume that there is information asymmetry between donors and recipients. Donors do not know recipients' private information, but the probability distribution of this information is common knowledge. Third, I expect the donors to be utility maximizers.

I begin by examining potential sources of demand for foreign aid, including the objectives of each of these sources. The literature indicates that there are two competing groups of motives for providing aid: recipients' needs and donors' interests (Maizels and Nissanke 1984). Recipients need foreign assistance to finance development, whereas donors may pursue their own political and economic interests in providing aid. I combine these two potentially competing groups of rationales into a form of enlightened donors' self-interest that recognizes that a world with less poverty and diseases and better-educated people is likely to provide a more secure and more stable environment with more opportunities for all of the world's population. In this regard, the sources of demand for foreign aid can be summarized as follows. First, citizens or taxpayers in donor countries have a real demand for foreign aid because they want to have an impact on development outcomes in developing countries because of a genuine desire to help the poor and a belief that spending a relatively small amount of tax money on promoting development can make the world more secure and save billions in security-related expenses. Second, businesses in the developed world have a demand for foreign aid to promote their exports. Evidence suggests that a large part of aid money is used to buy goods and services from donor countries. Therefore, donors are interested in maximizing the total impact of aid. This allows us to describe the foreign aid situation in terms of a principal–agent framework. One may assume that donors delegate to recipients the production of impact on development and transfer foreign aid in exchange.

Now consider a donor who wants to delegate to recipients the production of h units of impact on development outcomes. The value for the donor of these h units of impact is $H(h)$, where $H' > 0$, H'' 0, and $H(0) = 0$. The marginal value of the impact on development is thus positive and strictly decreasing with the number of units received by the donor. In terms of development outcomes, this impact could be an increase in per capita income and schooling, a reduction in poverty and maternal and infant mortality, and so on. The costs of recipients are not observable by the donor, but it is common knowledge that the marginal cost μ belongs to the set $M = \{\underline{\mu}, \bar{\mu}\}$. The recipient can be either efficient ($\underline{\mu}$) or inefficient ($\bar{\mu}$) with respective probabilities ρ and $1 - \rho$. I assume that the spread of uncertainty on the recipient's marginal cost is

$$\Delta\mu = \bar{\mu} - \underline{\mu} > 0. \qquad \text{(F.1)}$$

The variables of the problem considered thereafter are the impact produced (h) and the aid transfer (a) received by the recipient. Formally, there is a set of feasible allocations $A = \{h, a\}$. Suppose there is no information asymmetry between the donors and the recipients. The efficient allocation of the aid budget is obtained by equating the donors' marginal value of impact and the recipients' marginal cost. Hence, first-best allocation is obtained by the following first-order conditions:

$$H'(\underline{h}^*) = \underline{\mu} \text{ and} \qquad \text{(F.2)}$$

$$H'(\bar{h}^*) = \bar{\mu}. \qquad \text{(F.3)}$$

Because the donors' marginal value of impact is decreasing, the optimal impact levels defined by Equations F.2 and F.3 are such that $\underline{h}^* > \bar{h}$, that is, the optimal-level impact of an efficient recipient is greater than that of an inefficient recipient.

For successful delegation of the task, the donor must offer the agent a utility level that is as high as the utility level that the recipient obtains without receiving aid transfers. I normalize to zero the recipients' utility level without aid. Thus, the recipients' participation constraints can be formalized as

$$\underline{U} = \underline{a} - \underline{\mu}\underline{h} \geq 0 \text{ and} \tag{F.4}$$

$$\underline{U} = \bar{a} - \bar{\mu}\bar{h} \geq 0. \tag{F.5}$$

To implement the first-best aid allocation, in the complete information case, the donor can make the following take-it-or-leave-it offers to the recipient: if $\mu = \bar{\mu}$ (respectively, $\mu = \underline{\mu}$), the donor will offer the aid $\bar{a}$ (respectively, $\underline{a}$) for the impact level $\bar{h}^*$ (respectively, $\underline{h}^*$). In the complete information case the aid allocation model becomes similar to the model first developed by Dudley and Montmarquette (1976) and later extended by Trumbull and Wall (1994), which maximizes donors' utility given a budget constraint.

Now consider the case in which there is an information gap between donors and recipients. This information gap is due to the fungibility of aid and potential leakages of foreign assistance when donors and recipients have different objectives. The literature identifies two types of aid fungibility:

- Fungibility in the context of development or foreign aid refers to the recipients' ability to circumvent donor-imposed restrictions and spend some amount of the targeted aid on other programs.
- Fungibility in the context of public finance refers to the ability of an aid recipient to replace its own expenditures with aid transfers and to transform some portion of targeted aid into pure income or income-generating resources that can be spent in the way the recipient chooses (Devarajan and Swarup 1998).

When there is information asymmetry, inefficient recipients can mimic the efficient one and spend some amount of targeted aid on other activities. Therefore, a complete-information optimal aid allocation can no longer be implemented using asymmetric information. Using the language of incentive theory, one can say that complete-information aid allocation is not incentive compatible. That is why incentive compatibility constraints have to be added to the complete-information optimal aid allocation model. Further, with complete information, I assumed that donors are able to maintain all types of recipients at their zero status quo utility level. However, because donors want to allocate aid to all types of recipients, this will not be possible when there is information asymmetry. Inefficient recipients would get some information rent by mimicking an efficient recipient:

$$\underline{U} = \underline{a} - \underline{\mu}\bar{h} = \bar{a} - \bar{\mu}\bar{h} + \Delta\mu\bar{h} = \bar{U} + \Delta\mu\bar{h}, \tag{F.6}$$

where the first term is the zero status quo utility level of an efficient recipient and the second term is information rent coming from inefficient recipients' ability to mimic the efficient recipient. Because donors want to allocate some positive amount of aid to less efficient recipients, donors have to give up some positive information rent to relatively inefficient recipients. For simplicity, I denote the respective information rents of efficient and inefficient recipients as $\underline{U}$ and $\bar{U}$.

Now I can formalize donors' utility maximization problem. The respective expected utilities that a donor obtains from allocating aid to efficient and inefficient types of recipients are

$$\rho(H(\underline{h}) - \underline{a}) \text{ and } (1 - \rho)(H(\bar{h}) - \bar{a}).$$

The expected information rent can be written as

$$\rho\underline{U} + (1 - \rho)\bar{U}.$$

So donors will maximize the expected total utility from allocating aid between efficient and inefficient recipients minus the expected information rent of the recipients, that is,

$$\max_{a,h}\{\rho(H(\underline{h}) - \underline{a}) + (1 - \rho)(H(\bar{h}) - \bar{a})\} - \{\rho\underline{U} + (1 - \rho)\bar{U}\}, \quad \text{(F.7)}$$

subject to incentive compatibility, participation, and budget constraints.

The incentive compatibility constraints can be written as

$$\underline{a} - \underline{\mu}\underline{h} \geq \bar{a} - \underline{\mu}\bar{h} \text{ and} \quad \text{(F.8)}$$

$$\bar{a} - \bar{\mu}\bar{h} \geq \underline{a} - \bar{\mu}\underline{h}. \quad \text{(F.9)}$$

The participation constraints are the same as in Equations F.4 and F.5:

$$\underline{U} = \underline{a} - \underline{\mu}\underline{h} \geq 0 \text{ and}$$

$$\underline{U} = \bar{a} - \bar{\mu}\bar{h} \geq 0.$$

Finally, donors' total aid is constrained with the aid budget available:

$$\Sigma_j a_j = Y, \quad \text{(F.10)}$$

where Y is the total aid budget.

After some algebraic transformations, the first-order conditions for efficient recipients yield

$$H'(\underline{h}^*) = \underline{\mu}. \quad \text{(F.11)}$$

And maximization with respect to inefficient recipients yields

$$H'(\bar{h}^*) = \bar{\mu} + \frac{\rho}{1 - \rho}\Delta\mu. \quad \text{(F.12)}$$

The first-order conditions show that under asymmetric information, the optimal allocation of aid entails that there would be no distortion for efficient recipients with respect to complete information. There would be a downward distortion for inefficient recipients with Equation F.12.

The results just given indicate that any improvements in donors' information system will allow it to better maximize the utility they expect from the allocation of foreign aid; that is, improvements in donors' information structure increase their allocative efficiency. The idea here is to find signals that are exogenous to the aid allocation process. The informative signal will reduce information asymmetry and thus allow better aid allocation among recipients. The discussion in Chapter 2 of this book, which provides an overview of the literature on the relationship between governance and growth, clearly suggests that quality of governance is important in the development process.[1] Countries with high measures of political stability and accountability, less corrupt governments, and better protection of property rights are more likely to develop faster than countries with lower measures of political stability and accountability, more corruption, and poor property rights protection. Also, previous research identifies poor governance as a major reason for ineffective public spending (Mauro 1998; Abed and Gupta 2002; Rajkumar and Swaroop 2002). Because foreign assistance works similarly to public spending in many ways, some previous studies have shown that the lack of control for governance could plausibly lead to biased and inconsistent results regarding aid effectiveness. Therefore, I assume that donors could use quality of governance as an informative signal. Another way of reducing information asymmetry is to give less control over aid money to governments in countries with poor governance. This can be done by allocating aid to sectors or projects that are not under direct government control.

1. It is necessary to mention that there are some economists who support the reverse idea, namely growth in income and human capital causes institutional improvement. This line of research is most closely associated with the work of Seymour Martin Lipset (1960) and seems to accord well with the experiences of South Korea and Taiwan, which grew rapidly under one-party autocracies and eventually turned to democracy. Glaeser et al. (2004) is the most recent work in this line.

G Derivation of the Growth Equation Augmented with Human Capital

The derivation of the growth equation enhanced with human capital and governance is adapted from Bassanini and Scarpetta (2001) and Bassanini, Scarpetta, and Hemmings (2001). The standard neoclassical growth model augmented with human capital presents output at time t by the following constant return-to-scale production function with two inputs (capital and labor):

$$Y(t) = K(t)^{\alpha} H(t)^{\beta} (A(t)L(t))^{1-\alpha-\beta}, \tag{G.1}$$

where Y is output; L, K, and H are labor (population), physical capital, and human capital, respectively; A is level of technological and economic efficiency, and α and β are the partial elasticities of output with respect to physical and human capital. Assume that the level of economic and technological efficiency is determined by a combination of technological progress (W) and the quality of governance (G) (Bassanini, Scarpetta, and Hemmings [2001] assume that the second part is dependent on institutions and economic policy). The time path of the right-hand-side variables can be described as follows:

$$\dot{k}(t) = s_k(t)A(t)^{1-\alpha-\beta}k(t)^{\alpha}h(t)^{\beta} - (n(t) + d)k(t),$$

$$\dot{h}(t) = s_h(t)A(t)^{1-\alpha-\beta}k(t)^{\alpha}h(t)^{\beta} - (n(t) + d)h(t),$$

$$A(t) = G(t)\Omega(t),$$

$$\dot{A}(t) = g(t)A(t), \text{ and}$$

$$\dot{L}(t) = n(t)L(t), \tag{G.2}$$

where the dotted variables represent derivatives with respect to time; k and h are the capital/labor ratio and average human capital, respectively; s_k and s_h are

This derivation of the economic growth specification is based on Bassanini and Scarpetta (2001) and Bassanini, Scarpetta, and Hemmings (2001).

the investment rate in physical and human capital; and n and d stand for labor (population) growth and the depreciation rate.

Assuming that there are decreasing returns to reproducible factors (physical and human capital), that is, $\alpha + \beta < 1$, this system of equations can be solved to obtain steady-state values of k^* and h^* defined by

$$\ln k^*(t) = \ln A(t) + \frac{1-\beta}{1-\alpha-\beta}\ln s_k(t) + \frac{\beta}{1-\alpha-\beta}\ln s_h(t) - \frac{1}{1-\alpha-\beta}\ln(g(t)+n(t)+d) \quad \text{(G.3a)}$$

and

$$\ln h^*(t) = \ln A(t) + \frac{\alpha}{1-\alpha-\beta}\ln s_k(t) + \frac{1-\alpha}{1-\alpha-\beta}\ln s_h(t) - \frac{1}{1-\alpha-\beta}\ln(g(t)+n(t)+d), \quad \text{(G.3b)}$$

where ln is the natural log. Substituting Equations G.3a and G.3b into Equation G.1 and taking logs, we can obtain the following expression for the steady-state output in per capita terms (that is, $y = Y/L$):

$$\ln y^*(t) = \ln A(t) + \frac{\alpha}{1-\alpha}\ln s_k(t) + \frac{\beta}{1-\alpha}\ln h^*(t) - \frac{\alpha}{1-\alpha}\ln(g(t)+n(t)+d). \quad \text{(G.4)}$$

In this intensive form the steady-state output can be expressed either as a function of investment in human capital, s_h, or as a function of the steady-state stock of human capital, h^*. In this study human capital is approximated by secondary school enrollment and the average years of schooling of the population over the age 15. Therefore, Equation G.4 is expressed in terms of the stock of human capital.

However, h^* cannot be observed. Bassanini and Scarpetta (2001) establish a relationship between the steady-state stock of human capital and the actual level of human capital by solving the system of differential equations in Equation G.2 and substituting the investment rates in physical and human capital by Equation G.3. Suppressing the time subscript, we have

$$\frac{d\ln\frac{k}{A}}{dt} = (n+g+d)e^{-(1-\alpha)\ln\frac{k}{k^*}}e^{\beta\ln\frac{h}{h^*}} \text{ and} \quad \text{(G.5a)}$$

$$\frac{d\ln\frac{h}{A}}{dt} = (n+g+d)e^{\alpha\ln\frac{k}{k^*}}e^{-(1-\beta)\ln\frac{h}{h^*}}. \quad \text{(G.5b)}$$

Solving for $\ln h$, we obtain the following linearized form:

$$\ln(h(t)/A(t)) = \psi \ln(h^*(t)/A(t)) + (1 - \psi)\ln(h(t-1)/A(t-1)), \qquad \text{(G.6)}$$

where ψ is a function of α, β, and the term $(n + g + d)$. We can rearrange Equation G.6 to obtain the expression for h^* as a function of actual human capital:

$$\ln h^*(t) = \ln h(t) + \frac{1-\psi}{\psi}\Delta\ln(h(t)/A(t)). \qquad \text{(G.7)}$$

Substituting Equation G.7 into Equation G.4, the expression for steady-state output as a function of the investment rate and the actual stock of human capital can be obtained as

$$\ln y^*(t) = \ln A(t) + \frac{\alpha}{1-\alpha}\ln s_k(t) + \frac{\beta}{1-\alpha}(\ln h(t) + \frac{1-\psi}{\psi}$$

$$\Delta\ln(h(t)/A(t)) - \frac{\alpha}{1-\alpha}\ln(g(t) + n(t) + d). \qquad \text{(G.8)}$$

As stressed by Bassanini and Scarpetta (2001); Bassanini, Scarpetta, and Hemmings (2001); and other related empirical literature, the expression in Equation G.8 would be a valid specification of the growth equation if either one of the following two conditions were satisfied: (1) if countries were in their steady states and (2) if deviations from these steady states were independent and identically distributed. Otherwise, the transitional dynamics have to be modeled explicitly. Following Mankiw, Romer, and Weil (1992), the transitional dynamics can be expressed as

$$\frac{d\ln(y(t)/A(t))}{dt} = \lambda(\ln(y^*(t)/A(t)) - \ln(y(t)/A(t)), \qquad \text{(G.9)}$$

where $\lambda = (1 - \alpha - \beta(g(t) + n(t) + d)$.

Substituting the expressions for y^* and h^* into the solution of Equation G.9 yields the following expression:

$$\Delta\ln y(t) = -\phi(\lambda)\ln y(t-1) + \phi(\lambda)\frac{\alpha}{1-\alpha}\ln s_k(t) + \phi(\lambda)\frac{\beta}{1-\beta}\ln h(t)$$

$$+ \frac{1-\psi}{\psi}\frac{\beta}{1-\alpha}\Delta\ln h(t) - \phi(\lambda)\frac{\alpha}{1-\alpha}\ln(g + n(t) + d)$$

$$+ (1 - \frac{\phi(\lambda)}{\psi})g + \phi(\lambda)\ln A(0) + \phi(\lambda)gt. \qquad \text{(G.10)}$$

Because the level of technological progress and the quality of governance are not observable, they cannot be distinguished from the constant term empirically. However, we can proxy the quality of governance with the perceived level of governance. Therefore, an empirical specification of the growth equation can be expressed as follows:

$$\Delta \ln y(t) = a_0 + a_1 \ln y(t-1) + a_2 \ln s_k(t) + a_3 \ln h(t) + a_4 \Delta \ln h(t) + a_5 n(t) + a_6 t + a_7 G(t) + \xi(t), \qquad \text{(G.11)}$$

where

$$a_1 = -\phi(\lambda),$$

$$a_2 = \phi(\lambda)\frac{\alpha}{1-\alpha},$$

$$a_3 = \phi(\lambda)\frac{\beta}{1-\beta},$$

$$a_4 = \frac{1-\psi}{\psi}\frac{\beta}{1-\alpha},$$

$$a_5 = -\phi(\lambda)\frac{\alpha}{1-\alpha}.$$

Assuming that human capital is measured by school enrollment and that governance is measured by the perceived quality of governance and adding terms for control (X) and aid (A) variables, a simplified representation of the specification in Equation G.11 can be expressed as follows:

$$\text{Growth} = f(s_k, h, \Delta h, Gov, X, A). \qquad \text{(G.12)}$$

References

Abadie, A. 2005. "Poverty, Political Freedom, and the Roots of Terrorism." *American Economic Review* 95 (4): 50–56.

Abed, G. T., and S. Gupta, eds. 2002. *Governance, Corruption, and Economic Performance.* Washington, DC: International Monetary Fund.

Acemoglu, D., S. Johnson, and J. Robinson. 2001. "The Colonial Origins of Comparative Development: An Empirical Investigation." *American Economic Review* 91 (5): 1369–1401.

Agenor, P. R., and P. J. Montiel. 1996. *Development Macroeconomics.* Princeton, NJ, US: Princeton University Press.

Akyuz, Y., and A. Cornford. 1999. *Capital Flows to Developing Countries and the Reform of the International Financial System.* UNCTAD Discussion Paper 143. Geneva: United Nations Conference on Trade and Development.

Alesina, A., and D. Dollar. 2000. "Who Gives Foreign Aid to Whom and Why?" *Journal of Economic Growth* 5 (1): 33–63.

Alesina, A., and B. Weder. 1999. "Do Corrupt Governments Receive Less Foreign Aid?" *American Economic Review* 92 (4): 1126–1137.

Angrist, J., and J. S. Pischke. 2009. *Mostly Harmless Econometrics: An Empiricist's Companion.* Princeton, NJ, US: Princeton University Press.

Apodaca, C., and M. Stohl. 1999. "Human Rights Policy and Foreign Assistance." *International Studies Quarterly* 43 (1): 185–198.

Arellano, M. 2003. *Panel Data Econometrics.* Advanced Texts in Econometrics. New York: Oxford University Press.

Arellano, M., and S. Bond. 1991. "Some Tests of Specification for Panel Data: Monte Carlo Evidence and an Application to Employment Equations." *Review of Economic Studies* 58 (2): 277–297.

Arndt, C., and C. Oman. 2006. *Uses and Abuses of Governance Indicators.* Development Centre Study. Paris: Organization for Economic Cooperation and Development.

Arndt, C., S. Jones, and F. Tarp. 2010. "Aid, Growth, and Development: Have We Come Full Circle?" *Journal of Globalization and Development* 1 (2): Article 5.

Aschauer, D. A. 1989. "Does Public Capital Crowd Out Private Capital?" *Journal of Monetary Economics* 24 (2): 171–188.

———. 2000. "Public Capital and Economic Growth: Issues of Quantity, Finance, and Efficiency." *Economic Development and Cultural Change* 48 (2): 391–406.

Baldacci, E., B. Clements, S. Gupta, and Q. Cui. 2004. *Social Spending, Human Capital, and Growth in Developing Countries: Implications for Achieving the MDGs.* IMF Working Paper 04/217. Washington, DC: International Monetary Fund.

Barrett, C., and D. Maxwell. 2005. *Food Aid after Fifty Years: Recasting Its Role.* New York: Routledge.

Barro, R. J. 1996. *Determinants of Economic Growth: A Cross-Country Empirical Study.* NBER Working Paper 5968. Cambridge, MA, US: National Bureau of Economic Research.

Barro, R. J., and J. W. Lee. 2003. *International Data on Educational Attainment: Updates and Implications.* Center for International Development Working Paper 42. Cambridge, MA, US: Harvard University.

Bassanini, A., and S. Scarpetta. 2001. *Does Human Capital Matter for Growth in OECD Countries? Evidence from Pooled Mean Group Estimates.* OECD Economics Department Working Paper 282. Paris: Organisation for Economic Co-operation and Development.

Bassanini, A., S. Scarpetta, and P. Hemmings. 2001. *Economic Growth: The Role of Policies and Institutions.* OECD Economics Department Working Paper 283. Paris: Organisation for Economic Co-operation and Development.

Bauer, P. T. 1986. *Reality and Rhetoric: Studies in the Economics of Development.* Cambridge, MA, US: Harvard University Press.

Baum, C. F., M. E. Schaffer, and S. Stillman. 2007. "Enhanced Routines for Instrumental Variables/Generalized Method of Moments Estimation and Testing." *Stata Journal* 7 (4): 465–506.

Bazzi, S., and M. Clemens. 2009. *Blunt Instruments: On Establishing the Causes of Economic Growth.* CGD Working Paper 171. Washington, DC: Center for Global Development.

Bennell, P. 2002. "Hitting the Target: Doubling Primary School Enrollments in Sub-Saharan Africa by 2015." *World Developmen*t 30 (7): 1179–1194.

Berthélemy, J. C. 2006a. "Bilateral Donors' Interest vs. Recipients' Development Motives in Aid Allocation: Do All Donors Behave the Same?" *Review of Development Economics* 10 (2): 179–194.

———. 2006b. "Aid Allocation: Comparing Donors' Behaviors." *Swedish Economic Policy Review* 13 (2): 75–109.

Berthélemy, J. C., and A. Tichit. 2004. "Bilateral Donors' Aid Allocation Decisions—A Three Dimensional Panel Analysis." *International Review of Economics and Finance* 13 (3): 253–274.

Berthocchi, G., and F. Canova. 2002. "Did Colonization Matter for Growth? An Empirical Exploration into the Historical Causes of Africa's Underdevelopment." *European Economic Review* 46: 1851–1871.

Bhagwati, J. N. 1995. "The New Thinking on Development." *Journal of Democrac*y 6 (4): 50–64.

Bjórnskov, C. 2010. "Do Elites Benefit from Democracy and Foreign Aid in Developing Countries?" *Journal of Development Economics* 92: 115–124.

Blundell, R., and S. Bond. 1998. "Initial Conditions and Moment Conditions in Dynamic Panel Data Models." *Journal of Econometrics* 87: 115–143.

Boone, P. 1994. *The Impact of Foreign Aid on Savings and Growth.* Economics Working Paper. London: London School of Economics.

Bourguignon, F., and M. Sundberg. 2007. "Aid Effectiveness—Opening the Black Box." *American Economic Review* 97 (2): 316–321.

Burnside, C., and D. Dollar. 2000. "Aid, Policies, and Growth." *American Economic Review* 90 (4): 847–868.

———. 2004. "Aid, Policies, and Growth: Reply." *American Economic Review* 94 (3): 781–784.

Chenery, H. B. 1960. "Patterns of Industrial Growth." *American Economic Review* 50 (4): 624–654.

Chenery, H. B., and A. M. Strout. 1966. "Foreign Assistance and Economic Development." *American Economic Review* 66 (4): 679–703.

Chong, A., and M. Gradstein. 2008. "What Determines Foreign Aid? The Donors' Perspective." *Journal of Development Economics* 87 (1): 1–13.

Chow, G. 1993. "Capital Formation and Economic Growth in China." *Quarterly Journal of Economics* 108 (3): 809–842.

CIA (Central Intelligence Agency). 2011. *The World Factbook.* Accessed August 17. www.cia.gov/library/publications/the-world-factbook/.

Clemens, M. 2004. *The Long Walk to School: International Education Goals in Historical Perspective.* CGD Working Paper 37. Washington, DC: Center for Global Development.

Clemens, M., S. Radelet, and R. Bhavnani. 2004. *Counting Chickens When They Hatch: The Short Term Effect of Aid on Growth.* CGD Working Paper 44. Washington, DC: Center for Global Development.

Collier, P., and J. Dehn. 2001. *Aid, Shocks, and Growth.* Policy Research Working Paper 2688. Washington, DC: World Bank.

Collier, P., and D. Dollar. 2002. "Aid Allocation and Poverty Reduction." *European Economic Review* 46 (8): 1475–1500.

Collins, S. M., and B. P. Bosworth. 1996. "Economic Growth in East Asia: Accumulation versus Assimilation." *Brookings Papers on Economic Activity* 2: 135–203.

Cordella, T., and G. Dell'Ariccia. 2003. *Budget Support versus Project Aid.* IMF Working Paper 03/88. Washington, DC: International Monetary Fund.

Cragg, J. G., and S. G. Donald. 1993. "Testing Identifiability and Specification in Instrumental Variables Models." *Econometric Theory* 9: 222–240.

Dalgaard, C. J., and H. Hansen. 2000. *On Aid, Growth, and Good Policies.* CREDIT Research Paper. Nottingham, UK: University of Nottingham, Centre for Research in Economic Development and International Trade.

Dalgaard, C. J., H. Hansen, and F. Tarp. 2004. "On the Empirics of Foreign Aid and Growth." *Economic Journal* 114 (June): F191–F216.

Deaton, A. 1997. *Analysis of Household Surveys: A Microeconometric Approach to Development Policy.* Baltimore: Johns Hopkins University Press.

Deaton, A. 2009. *Instruments of Development: Randomization in the Tropics, and the Search for the Elusive Keys to Economic Development.* NBER Working Paper 14690. Cambridge, MA, US: National Bureau of Economic Research.

de Mesquita, B. B., and A. Smith. 2009. "A Political Economy of Aid." *International Organization* 63 (2): 309–340.

Dervis, K., J. de Melo, and S. Robinson. 1982. *General Equilibrium Models for Development Policy.* New York: Cambridge University Press.

Desmet, K., I. Ortuño-Ortin, and R. Wacziarg. 2009. *The Political Economy of Ethno-*

linguistic Cleavages. NBER Working Paper 15360. Cambridge, MA, US: National Bureau of Economic Research.

Devarajan, S., and V. Swarup. 1998. *The Implications of Foreign Aid Fungibility for Development Assistance.* Policy Research Working Paper 2022. Washington, DC: World Bank.

DFID (UK Department for International Development). 2000. *Halving World Poverty by 2015: Economic Growth, Equity and Security.* London.

Dixit, A. 2009. "Governance Institutions and Economic Activity." *American Economic Review* 99 (1): 5–24.

Dollar, D., and W. Easterly. 1999. "The Search for the Key: Aid, Investment, and Policies in Africa." *Journal of African Economies* 8 (4): 546–577.

Dollar, D., and V. Levin. 2004. *The Increasing Selectivity of Foreign Aid, 1984–2002.* Policy Research Working Paper 3299. Washington, DC: World Bank.

Dreber, A., P. Nunnenkamp, and R. Thiele. 2008. "Does Aid for Education Educate Children? Evidence from Panel Data." *World Bank Economic Review* 22 (2): 291–314.

Drèze, J., and A. Sen. 2002. *India: Development and Participation.* New Delhi: Oxford University Press.

Dudley, L., and C. Montmarquette. 1976. "A Model of the Supply of Bilateral Foreign Aid." *American Economic Review* 66 (1): 132–142.

Duflo, E., and M. Kremer. 2005. "Use of Randomization in the Evaluation of Development Effectiveness." In *Evaluating Development Effectiveness,* vol. 7, edited by O. Feinstein, G. K. Ingram, and G. K. Pitman, 205–232. London: Transaction.

Durbarry, R., N. Gemmell, and D. Greenaway. 1998. *New Evidence on the Impact of Foreign Aid on Economic Growth.* Credit Research Paper 98-8. Nottingham, UK: University of Nottingham, Centre for Research in Economic Development and International Trade.

Durlauf, S. N., P. A. Johnson, and J. R. W. Temple. 2005. "Growth Econometrics." In *Handbook of Economic Growth,* vol. 1, edited by A. P. Aghion and S. Durlauf, 555–677. London: Elsevier.

Easterly, W. 2003. "Can Foreign Aid Buy Growth?" *Journal of Economic Perspectives* 17 (3): 23–48.

———. 2006. *The White Man's Burden: Why the West's Efforts to Aid the Rest Have Done So Much Ill and So Little Good.* New York: Oxford University Press.

———. 2007. "Was Development Assistance a Mistake?" *American Economic Review* 97 (2): 328–332.

Easterly, W., and T. Pfutze. 2008. "Where Does the Money Go? Best and Worst Practices in Foreign Aid." *Journal of Economic Perspectives* 22 (2): 29–52.

Easterly, W., R. Levine, and D. Roodman. 2004. "Aid, Policies, and Growth: Comment." *American Economic Review* 94 (3): 774–780.

Fan, S. 2008. *Public Expenditures, Growth, and Poverty: Lessons from Developing Countries.* Baltimore: Johns Hopkins University Press.

Fedderke, J., R. Klitgaard, and K. Akramov. 2005. "Heterogeneity Happens: How Rights Matter in Economic Development." Manuscript. Pardee RAND Graduate School, Santa Monica, CA, USA.

Fei, J. C. H., and G. Ranis. 1964. *Development of the Labor Surplus Economy: Theory and Policy.* Homewood, IL, US: Richard A. Irwin.

Feng, Y. 2004. *Democracy, Governance, and Economic Performance: Theory and Evidence.* Cambridge, MA, US: MIT Press.

Fischer, S. 1993. "Role of Macroeconomic Factors in Growth." *Journal of Monetary Economics* 32 (3): 485–512.

Fleck, R. K., and C. Kilby. 2010. "Changing Aid Regimes? U.S. Foreign Aid from the Cold War to the War on Terror." *Journal of Development Economics* 91: 185–197.

Frankel, J. A., and D. Romer. 1999. "Does Trade Cause Growth?" *American Economic Review* 89 (3): 379–399.

Freedom House. 2009. Freedom in the World Country Ratings database. Washington, DC.

Friedman, M. 1958. "Foreign Economic Aid: Means and Objectives." *Yale Review* 47 (4): 500–515.

Gartzke, E. 1998. "Kant We All Get Along? Opportunity, Willingness, and the Origins of the Democratic Peace." *American Journal of Political Science* 42 (1): 1–27.

———. 2010. The Affinity of Nations: Similarity of State Voting Positions in the UN General Assembly database. Accessed August 22, 2011. http://dss.ucsd.edu/~egartzke/htmlpages/data.html.

Glaeser, E., R. La Porta, F. L. de Silanes, and A. Shleifer. 2004. *Do Institutions Cause Growth?* NBER Working Paper 10568. Cambridge, MA, US: National Bureau of Economic Research.

Grier, R. M. 1999. "Colonial Legacies and Economic Growth." *Public Choice* 98: 317–335.

Guillaumont, P., and L. Chauvet. 2001. "Aid and Performance: A Reassessment." *Journal of Development Studies* 37 (6): 66–92.

Hadjimichael, M. T., D. Ghura, M. Mühleisen, R. Nord, and E. M. Ucer. 1995. *Sub-Saharan Africa: Growth, Savings, and Investment, 1986–93.* IMF Occasional Paper 118. Washington, DC: International Monetary Fund.

Hall, R. E., and C. I. Jones. 1999. "Why Do Some Countries Produce So Much More Output per Worker than Others?" *Quarterly Journal of Economics* 114 (1): 83–116.

Hansen, H., and F. Tarp. 2000. "Aid Effectiveness Disputed." In *Foreign Aid and Development,* edited by F. Tarp, 103–128. London and New York: Routledge.

———. 2001. "Aid and Growth Regressions." *Journal of Development Economics* 64 (2): 547–570.

Harris, J. R., and M. P. Todaro. 1970. "Migration, Unemployment, and Development: A Two Sector Analysis." *American Economic Review* 60 (1): 126–142.

Heckelman, J., and S. Knack. 2008. "Foreign Aid and Market-Liberalizing Reforms." *Economica* 75: 524–548.

Heston, A., R. Summers, and B. Aten. 2009. Penn World Table Version 6.3. Accessed August 22, 2011. http://pwt.econ.upenn.edu/php_site/pwt_index.php.

Hjertholm, P., and H. White. 2000. "Foreign Aid in Historical Perspective: Background and Trend." In *Foreign Aid and Development,* by P. Hjertholm and H. White, 80–102. London: Routledge.

Hodler, R. 2007. "Rent Seeking and Aid Effectiveness." *International Tax and Public Finance* 14: 525–541.

Hoff, K., A. Braverman, and J. Stiglitz, eds. 1993. *Economics of Rural Organization: Theory, Practice, and Policy.* New York: Oxford University Press.

Hymer, S. H., and S. Resnick. 1969. "A Model of Agrarian Economy with Non-agricultural Activity." *American Economic Review* 59 (4): 493–506.

IDA (International Development Association). 2007. *Aid Architecture: An Overview of the Main Trends in Official Development Assistance Flows.* Washington, DC: World Bank.

IMF (International Monetary Fund). 2006. Directions of Trade Statistics (DOTS) database. Washington, DC. CD-ROM.

Islam, N. 1995. "Growth Empirics: A Panel Data Approach." *Quarterly Journal of Economics* 110 (4): 1127–1170.

Johnston, B. F., and P. Kilby. 1975. *Agriculture and Structural Transformation: Economic Strategies in Late-Developing Countries.* New York: Oxford University Press.

Jütting, J. 2003. *Institutions and Development: A Critical Review.* OECD Development Centre Working Paper 210. Paris: Organisation for Economic Co-operation and Development.

Kanbur, R. 2000. "Aid, Conditionality, and Debt in Africa." In *Foreign Aid and Development,* edited by F. Tarp, 409–422. London: Routledge.

———. 2006. "The Economics of International Aid." In *The Economics of Giving, Reciprocity, and Altruism,* edited by J. M. Ythier, S. C. Kolm, and L. A. Gerard-Varet. New York: Palgrave Macmillan.

Kaufmann, D., and A. Kraay. 2002. *Governance Matters.* Policy Research Working Paper 2196. Washington, DC: World Bank.

Kaufmann, D., A. Kraay, and P. Zoido-Lobaton. 1999. *Aggregating Governance Indicators.* Policy Research Working Paper 2195. Washington, DC: World Bank.

———. 2003. *Governance Matters, III.* Policy Research Working Paper 3106. Washington, DC: World Bank.

Kleibergen, F., and R. Paap. 2006. "Generalized Reduced Rank Tests Using the Singular Value Decomposition." *Journal of Econometrics* 127: 97–126.

Klitgaard, R., J. Fedderke, and K. Akramov. 2005. "Choosing and Using Performance Criteria." In *High-Performance Government: Structure, Leadership, Incentives,* edited by R. Klitgaard and P. C. Light, 407–446. Santa Monica, CA, US: RAND Corporation.

Knack, S. 2000. *Aid Dependence and the Quality of Governance: A Cross-Country Empirical Analysis.* Policy Research Working Paper 2396. Washington, DC: World Bank.

Knack, S., and A. Rahman. 2007. "Donor Fragmentation and Bureaucratic Quality in Aid Recipients." *Journal of Development Economics* 83 (1): 176–197.

Kosack, S. 2003. "Effective Aid: How Democracy Allows Development Aid to Improve the Quality of Life." *World Development* 31 (1): 1–22.

Kourtellos, A., C. M. Tan, and X. Zhang. 2007. "Is the Relationship between Aid and Economic Growth Nonlinear?" *Journal of Macroeconomics* 29 (3): 515–540.

Krueger, A. B., and J. Malečková. 2003. "Education, Poverty and Terrorism: Is There a Causal Connection?" *Journal of Economic Perspectives* 17 (4): 119–144.

Krugman, P. 1994. "The Myth of Asia's Miracle." *Foreign Affairs* 73 (1): 62–78.

Kuznets, S. 1966. *Modern Economic Growth.* New Haven, CT, US: Yale University Press.

Laffont, J. J., and D. Martimort. 2002. *The Theory of Incentives: The Principal-Agent Model.* Princeton, NJ, US: Princeton University Press.

Lensink, R., and O. Morrissey. 2000. "Aid Instability as a Measure of Uncertainty and the Positive Impact of Aid on Growth." *Journal of Development Studies* 36 (3): 31–49.

Lensink, R., and H. White. 2001. "Are There Negative Returns to Aid?" *Journal of Development Studies* 37 (1): 42–65.

Levine, R., and D. Renelt. 1992. "A Sensitivity Analysis of Cross-Country Growth Regressions." *American Economic Review* 82 (4): 942–963.

Levy, V. 1987. "Does Concessionary Aid Lead to Higher Investment Rates in Low-Income Countries?" *Review of Economics and Statistics* 69 (1): 152–156.

Little, I. M. D., and J. Clifford. 1965. *International Aid.* London: Allen and Unwin.

Little, I. M. D., and J. A. Mirrlees. 1974. *Project Appraisal and Planning.* London: Heinemann.

Lucas, R. E., Jr. 1988. "On the Mechanics of Economic Development." *Journal of Monetary Economics* 22 (1): 3–42.

Maizels, A., and M. Nissanke. 1984. "Motivations for Aid to Developing Countries." *World Development* 12 (9): 879–900.

Mankiw, G. N., D. Romer, and D. N. Weil. 1992. "A Contribution to the Empirics of Economic Growth." *Quarterly Journal of Economics* 107 (2): 407–437.

Marshall, M. G., K. Jaggers, and T. R. Gurr. 2010. Polity IV Project: Political Regime Characteristics and Transitions, 1800–2010. Accessed at various times in 2010. www.systemicpeace.org/polity/polity4.htm.

Mauro, P. 1996. *The Effects of Corruption on Growth, Investment, and Government Expenditure.* IMF Working Paper 96/98. Washington, DC: International Monetary Fund.

———. 1998. "Corruption and the Composition of Government Expenditure." *Journal of Public Economics* 69 (2): 263–279.

Mavrotas, G. 2003. *Assessing Aid Effectiveness in Uganda: An Aid-Disaggregation Approach.* Oxford, UK: Oxford Policy Management.

McGillivray, M. 2004. "Descriptive and Prescriptive Analyses of Aid Allocation: Approaches, Issues, and Consequences." *International Review of Economics and Finance* 13 (3): 275–292.

McGillivray, M., and O. Morrissey. 2000. "Aid Fungibility in *Assessing Aid:* Red Herring or True Concern?" *Journal of International Development* 12 (3): 413–428.

Miguel, E., and M. Kremer. 2004. "Worms: Identifying Impacts on Education and Health in the Presence of Treatment Externalities." *Econometrica* 72 (1): 159–217.

Minoiu, C., and S. G. Reddy. 2009. *Developmental Aid and Economic Growth: A Positive Long-Run Relation.* IMF Working Paper 09/118. Washington, DC: International Monetary Fund.

Mishra, P., and D. Newhouse. 2009. "Does Health Aid Matter?" *Journal of Health Economics* 28 (4): 855–872.

Mobarak, A. M. 2005. "Democracy, Volatility, and Economic Development." *Review of Economics and Statistics* 87 (2): 348–361.

Mosley, P., J. Hudson, and S. Horrel. 1987. "Aid, the Public Sector, and the Market in Less Developed Countries." *Economic Journal* 97 (2): 616–641.

———. 1992. "Aid, the Public Sector and the Market in Less Developed Countries: A Return to the Scene of the Crime." *Journal of International Development* 4 (2): 139–150.

Neumayer, E. 2003. *The Pattern of Aid Giving: The Impact of Good Governance on Development Assistance.* London: Routledge Studies in Development Economics.

North, D. 1990. *Institutions, Institutional Change, and Economic Performance.* New York: Cambridge University Press.

Nunn, N. 2007. "Historical Legacies: A Model Linking Africa's Past to Its Current Underdevelopment." *Journal of Development Economics* 83: 157–175.

Nurkse, R. 1953. *Problems of Capital Formation in Underdeveloped Countries.* New York: Oxford University Press.

OECD (Organisation for Economic Co-operation and Development). 2007. *Reporting Directives for the Credit Reporting System.* Paris.

———. 2011. "Development Aid Reaches an Historic High in 2010." Accessed August 18. www.oecd.org/document/35/0,3746,en_2649_34447_47515235_1_1_1_1,00.html.

———. Various years a. Development Database on Aid Activities: CRS Online. Accessed August 16, 2011. www.oecd.org/document/0/0,2340,en_2649_34447_37679488_1_1_1_1,00.html.

———. Various years b. Development Database on Aid from DAC (Development Assistance Committee) Members: DAC Online. Accessed August 16, 2011. www.oecd.org/document/33/0,2340,en_2649_34447_36661793_1_1_1_1,00.html.

OED (*Oxford English Dictionary*). 2011. *Oxford English Dictionary* Online. Accessed January 17, 2012. www.oed.com.

Ovaska, T. 2003. "The Failure of Development Aid." *Cato Journal* 23 (2): 175–188.

Owens, T., and J. Hoddinott. 1999. *Investing in Development or Investing in Relief: Quantifying the Poverty Tradeoffs Using Zimbabwe Household Panel Data.* CSAE Working Paper 99/4. Oxford, UK: Oxford University, Centre for the Study of African Economies.

PRS Group Inc. 2011. "International Country Risk Guide Methodology." Accessed November 29. www.prsgroup.com/PDFS/icrgmethodology.pdf.

Przeworski, A., M. E. Alvarez, J. A. Cheibub, and F. Limongi. 2000. *Democracy and Development: Political Institutions and Well-Being in the World, 1950–1990.* Cambridge, UK: Cambridge University Press.

Quibria, M. G. 2005. "Rethinking Aid Effectiveness: Facts, Issues and Policies." *World Economics* 6 (1): 101–117.

Radelet, S. 2006. *A Primer on Foreign Aid.* CGD Working Paper 92. Washington, DC: Center for Global Development.

Radelet, S., M. Clemens, and R. Bhavnani. 2005. "Aid and Growth." *Finance and Development* 42 (3): 1–13.

Rajan, R. G., and A. Subramanian. 2005. *What Undermines Aid's Impact on Growth?* IMF Working Paper 05/126. Washington, DC: International Monetary Fund.

———. 2007. "Does Aid Affect Governance?" *American Economic Review* 97 (2): 322–327.

———. 2008. "Aid and Growth: What Does the Cross-Country Evidence Really Show?" *Review of Economics and Statistics* 90 (4): 643–665.

Rajkumar, A. S., and V. Swaroop. 2008. "Public Spending and Outcomes: Does Governance Matter?" *Journal of Development Economics* 86 (1): 96–111.

Ravallion, M., and S. Chen. 2003. "Measuring Pro-poor Economic Growth." *Economic Letters* 78 (1): 93–99.

Remmer, K. 2004. "Does Foreign Aid Promote the Expansion of Government?" *American Journal of Political Science* 48: 77–92.

Rivera-Batiz, F. L. 2002. "Democracy, Governance, and Economic Growth: Theory and Evidence." *Review of Development Economics* 6 (2): 225–247.

Rodrik, D., A. Subramanian, and F. Trebbi. 2004. "Institutions Rule: The Primacy of Institutions over Geography and Integration in Economic Development." *Journal of Economic Growth* 9 (2): 131–165.

Roodman, D. 2006. *How to Do xtabond2: An introduction to "Difference" and "System" GMM in Stata.* CGD Working Paper 103. Washington, DC: Center for Global Development.

———. 2007. *Macro Aid Effectiveness Research: A Guide for the Perplexed.* CGD Working Paper 134. Washington, DC: Center for Global Development.

Rose, A. K. 2004. "Do We Really Know That the WTO Increases Trade?" *American Economic Review* 94 (1): 98–114.

Sachs, J. D. 2005. *The End of Poverty: Economic Possibilities for Our Time.* New York: Penguin.

Sala-i-Martin, X., G. Doppelhofer, and R. I. Miller. 2004. "Determinants of Long-Term Growth: A Bayesian Averaging of Classical Estimates (BACE)." *American Economic Review* 94 (4): 813–835.

Schweinberger, A. G., and S. Lahiri. 2006. "On the Provision of Official and Private Foreign Aid." *Journal of Development Economics* 80: 179–197.

Staiger, D., and J. Stock. 1997. "Instrumental Variables Regression with Weak Instruments." *Econometrica* 65 (3): 557–586.

Stern, N. 2002. *Strategy for Development.* Washington, DC: World Bank.

Stiglitz, J. 2002. "Participation and Development: Perspectives from the Comprehensive Development Paradigm." *Review of Development Economics* 6 (2): 163–182.

Svensson, J. 2000a. "When Is Foreign Aid Policy Credible? Aid Dependence and Conditionality." *Journal of Development Economics* 61 (1): 61–84.

———. 2000b. "Foreign Aid and Rent-Seeking." *Journal of International Economics* 51 (2): 437–461.

Thorbecke, E. 2000. "The Evolution of the Development Doctrine and the Role of Foreign Aid, 1950–2000." In *Foreign Aid and Development: Lessons Learnt and Directions for the Future,* edited by F. Tarp, 17–47. London: Routledge.

Tooley, J., and P. Dixon. 2006. "The Failures of State Schooling in Developing Countries and the People's Response." In *2006 Index of Economic Freedom,* edited by M. Miles, K. R. Holmes, and M. A. O'Grady, 27–37. Washington, DC: Heritage Foundation and Wall Street Journal.

Trumbull, W. N., and H. Wall. 1994. "Estimating Aid Allocation Criteria with Panel Data." *Economic Journal* 104 (425): 876–882.

UNDP (United Nations Development Programme). 1997. *Reconceptualizing Governance.* New York.

UNESCAP (United Nations Economic and Social Commission for Asia and Pacific). 2006. *Achieving MDGs in Asia: A Case for More Aid.* Bangkok, Thailand.

USAID (United States Agency for International Development). 2002. *Foreign Aid in the National Interest: Promoting Freedom, Security, and Opportunity.* Washington, DC.

Van de Sijpe, N. 2010. *Is Foreign Aid Fungible? Evidence from the Education and Health Sectors.* CSAE Working Paper 38. Oxford, UK: Oxford University, Centre for the Study of African Economies.

Wacziarg, R., and K. H. Welch. 2003. *Trade Liberalization and Growth: New Evidence.* NBER Working Paper 10152. Cambridge, MA, US: National Bureau of Economic Research.

Watkins, K. 2000. *Oxfam Education Report.* London: Oxfam Publishing.
White, H. 1992. "Macroeconomic Impact of Development Aid." *Journal of Development Studies* 28 (2): 163–240.
———. 1998. *Aid and Macroeconomic Performance.* London: Macmillan.
———. 2004. "Trends in the Volume and Allocation of Official Flows from Donor Countries." *International Review of Economics and Finance* 13 (3): 233–244.
Windmeijer, F. 2005. "A Finite Sample Correction for the Variance of Linear Efficient Two-Step GMM Estimators." *Journal of Econometrics* 126: 25–51.
Wolfensohn, J., and F. Bourguignon. 2004. *Development and Poverty Reduction: Looking Back, Looking Ahead.* Washington, DC: World Bank.
Wooldridge, J. M. 2002. *Econometric Analysis of Cross Section and Panel Data.* Cambridge, MA, US: MIT Press.
World Bank. 1993. *The East Asian Miracle: Economic Growth and Public Policy.* Washington, DC.
———. 1998. *Assessing Aid: What Works, What Doesn't, and Why?* Washington, DC.
———. 2007. *World Development Report 2008: Agriculture for Development.* New York: Oxford University Press.
———. 2010. World Development Indicators (WDI) database. Accessed August 26, 2011. http://databank.worldbank.org/ddp/home.do?Step=12&id=4&CNO=2.
———. 2012. *Global Development Finance: External Debt of Developing Countries.* Washington, DC.
Younas, J. 2008. "Motivation for Bilateral Aid Allocation: Altruism or Trade Benefits." *European Journal of Political Economy* 24 (3): 661–674.
Young, A. 1995. "The Tyranny of Numbers: Confronting the Statistical Realities of the East Asian Growth Experience." *Quarterly Journal of Economics* 110 (3): 641–680.

Index

Page numbers for entries occurring in figures are followed by an *f;* those for entries in notes, by an *n;* and those for entries in tables, by a *t.*

About the Author

Kamiljon T. Akramov is a research fellow in the Development Strategy and Governance Division of the International Food Policy Research Institute, Washington, DC.